# 1001
## IMAGES OF
# HORSES

TEXT BY BERTRAND LECLAIR

**CRESCENT BOOKS**
**NEW YORK • AVENEL, NEW JERSEY**

# CONTENTS

CLB 2897
© 1992 Colour Library Books Ltd., Godalming, Surrey, England.
This 1992 edition published by Crescent Books,
Distributed by Outlet Book Company, Inc., a Random House Company,
40 Engelhard Avenue, Avenel, New Jersey, 07001
Printed and bound in Singapore
All rights reserved
ISBN 0 517 06943 1
8 7 6 5 4 3 2 1

# FOREWORD

*T*he story of mankind's unique partnership with the horse drifts back into the dim dark ages of antiquity. One cannot resist pondering on where we might be today without his influence and help. What price the invention of the wheel, for example, without the horse to pull the cart or carriage? How could we have fed our rapidly increasing population without his help in sowing the land and reaping the harvest? And what of transport and communications – so essential to the development of our civilisation and yet impossible without his help.

*It is difficult to envisage just where or how mankind would have developed without the horse. Our partnership with him bridges the awesome gap in our history between the invention of the wheel and the steam and combustion engine.*

*Once our partner in peace and war, toil and pleasure, his role today is almost exclusively consigned to the latter.*

*The symbol of wide open spaces and freedom, synonymous with nature in a mechanised world, the horse arouses great passion and feeds our imaginations. Who has not dreamt of some mad race along a deserted beach, the wind and spray in your face, as you gallop in wild abandonment? What child has not dreamt of sharing his secrets and problems with his pony, a warm and comforting best friend?*

*Riffling through these pages at random and letting your imagination be caught by some wonderful picture, you suddenly realise how many facets there are to the horse – as varied as life itself. The pet at the bottom of your garden is a direct descendant of the primitive equus, evolved in the freedom of the Russian steppes, as is the gentle giant of a work horse hauling its daily load of heavy logs, the film star, or the little black pony tearing round jump after jump. Every horse is unique but every one brings us close to nature. Browsing through this book will show you the powerful attractions of the many different breeds, or if you are already an experienced and knowledgeable horseman you may well discover new exciting activites you were not previously familiar with.*

*The purpose of this book is not to indulge in learned scientific discussion or to produce yet another manual of horsemanship, but to open a doorway into the wonderful world of the horse and all his myriad activities throughout the world today.*

*This remarkable collection of carefully selected photographs – backed by a concise yet comprehensive text – guides the reader on this rewarding journey, guaranteeing the maximum pleasure with the minimum effort. Its intention is to whet the appetite and lead the enthusiast – either as spectator or paricipant – into areas they may not previously have considered. Here is the horse in all his guises and all his glory – god bless him!*

# WILD HORSES

# THE PRZEWALSKI AND THE TARPAN — PREHISTORIC BREEDS SURVIVE

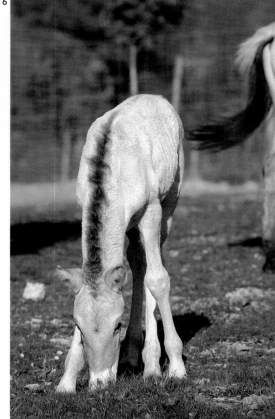

**L**ike all animals, the horse started life as a wild and free creature. Man, in seven or eight thousand years of domesticating the horse has, through breeding and working horses, succeeded in producing many changed breeds. However, two original, primitive breeds have survived to the present day. Direct descendants of the Equus, ancient common ancestor of all the family of equides (horse, donkey and zebra, defined by their single-toed foot or hoof), the Tarpan and the Przewalski retain the characteristics of the first horse: a heavy head with a convex profile, short canon bones, narrow quarters and, occasionally, zebra marks on the legs. They share with the zebra and some ancient breeds of pony, (including the Fjord) a spiky mane.

They also bear a striking resemblance to the horses seen in the prehistoric cave paintings at Lascaux, in France.

The Przewalski horse, standing between 13 and 14.2 hands, lives on the steppes of Mongolia on the edge of the Gobi Desert. Its isolation in a desert region, its hardiness and the aggressiveness of its stallions, explain why it has barely evolved since the ice age. It was discovered by the explorer Nicolai Przewalski in 1881 and was long hunted for its meat, but today, as an example of the original horse, it benefits from protection in the wild as well as being sheltered in zoos throughout the world. Considered to be the founder of most modern breeds, the Przewalski horse is the direct ancestor of the Mongolian pony used by the Nomad tribes of that country as a work horse.

The wild Tarpan owes its survival only to a revival of breeding in semi-captivity. In Poland and Russia, where it was hunted for meat and broken for work this small horse (14 hands) nearly became extinct at the end of the 19th century. Careful selection for breeding and protection of the survivors has allowed the breed characteristics to be preserved and scientists are, today, studying the behaviour of Tarpans in the forest of Popielno in Poland. The Tarpan is one of the original breeds from which many European breeds are descended; being used as a war horse it travelled with the great Celtic invasions at the dawn of civilisation.

The Prezwalski horse stands between 13 and 14.2 hands. The small size is typical of primitive breeds, as is the heavy head with its convex profile, straight shoulders, flat withers, wide body and short canon bones. It is usually light bay or dun coloured, with a spiky mane and no forelock

The Tarpan also stands between 13 and 14.2 hands with lightweight quarters. Colouring varies from grey to dark bay and it often has a stripe mark down the spine (14) and zebra markings on the legs (8). Its mane sometimes sticks up, sometimes not (3, 5, 7, 8, 14).

# THE CAMARGUE: WHITE MANED HORSE OF THE SEAS

The small grey horses which live in the marshes of the Rhône delta surrounded by the Mediterranean, are the mysterious subject of many myths. Scientists are in agreement that the breed goes back to prehistoric times; the Camargue horse is a descendant of the prehistoric horse of Solutré, its morphology being very close to that of the fossilised remains of prehistoric horses found at Solutré in France, dating from the upper palaeolithic period. The geographical isolation of the Camargue has preserved it from cross breeding whilst natural selection, as a result of the difficult terrain of reeds and sea grasses which form its habitat, has created a small, stocky, sure-footed animal whose adult colouring is nearly always grey (foals are born with a dark coat). Their habitat has also resulted in a herd life peculiar to themselves which has been the subject of rich scientific research. A *manade* (the Provençal name for a herd of horses), set free and given total autonomy, has been under close observation by researchers for the past twenty years. This study has produced precious information on the social structure of horses in general and their faculty of adaptation. It was found that faults of inbreeding are very few, thanks to natural selection, and that the hierarchy among mares in the heart of a harem is firmly established: the youngest submits to the eldest, regardless of the latter's physical weakness. It has also been seen that the natural eating habits of these horses have proved very beneficial to the local ecosystems.

Generally the Camargue horse, today as yesterday, lives in a semi-wild state in the region where it originated, in herds looked after by the famous "guardians" of the Camargue. These men continue to breed horses for cattle work and operate a selection system (the least good looking of the young stallions being castrated in an annual round up), thus improving the breed. Its sure-footedness, sturdiness and gentle temperament once schooled, make the Camargue an excellent riding horse. Its hardiness and agility fit it particularly well for trekking, where its small size and sensible temperament are particularly appreciated by novice riders. Camargue horses are also bred outside the region.

10

7

11

Camargue foals are born with a dark coat which gets lighter as they grow, finally becoming a light grey. Powerfully built but small (13.1-14.1 hands), the size of a large pony, the Camargue has solid legs adapted to its marshy habitat. It spends most of its time looking for feed in a sparse environment for a grass eater. Spring is the time for battles between the stallions and these often end in serious damage which, however, heals spectacularly without human help.

8

12

15

9

13

16

14

# THE MUSTANG AND THE BRUMBY: FREEDOM REGAINED

When the first Europeans landed on the shores of America the horse had not been seen on that continent since the ice age. Nevertheless America, like Australia, has its wild horses.

The American Mustang, in direct contrast to the breeds discussed above, is descended from domesticated horses brought into the country in the 16th century by the Spanish conquistadors and returned to the wild. The mustang has retained traces of its Iberian ancestry in a family resemblance to the Andalusian and Barbary horses from which it is descended. But three centuries of freedom, of natural reproduction without interference by man, has resulted in a weakening of the breed, made worse by the fact that the best specimens were captured by firstly Indians and then cowboys. The latter began very early on to round up the hardy and agile Mustangs to train as cattle horses. This is why Mustang blood runs in all North American breeds of horse, from the Appaloosan and Palomino to the Quarter Horse. Today the last of the wild herds are protected by the government and breed registers are kept of Mustangs considered to carry the characteristics of their origins. Once schooled they are particularly suitable for trail riding and endurance riding.

The Australian Brumby, a distant cousin of the Mustang, is not lucky enough to be protected; on the contrary man is its worst enemy. This Australian bush horse, with no obvious breed characteristics, is the descendant of riding horses abandoned at the time of the great 19th century gold rushes. The exceptionally severe Australian climate and environment have brought about rigorous natural selection in which only the strongest and hardiest survive. Up until the middle of this century, the Brumby continued to be rounded up to work on the land, but mechanisation having supervened they are now simply considered pests in a country of large scale farming. Hunted and killed and extremely wary of man, they are becoming harder and harder to domesticate. Societies for the protection of animals try to fight against the remorseless hunting down of this creature – once man's faithful servant in the conquest of new lands and now thrown on the scrapheap of history.

6

9

10

14

7

11 The Mustang's antecedents are too complicated for there to be a typical Mustang type, but generally they are not large horses (under 16 hands). They often have a hollow back and heavy legs. They may be any colour from dun to spotted. All American breeds are descended from Mustangs who have passed on to them some Andalusian blood (1 to 13).

Distant cousins of the Mustang can be found in the wild in Spain, as the Andalusian has returned to a semi-wild state in the great Donana reserve of their native country (14 & 15).

8

12

13

15

# COMPANION HORSES

# KEEPING A HORSE AT HOME

**M**any people dream of keeping a horse at home; a friend and pet who will be part of the family, steaming up the kitchen window as he presses his nose against it to ask for his apple or lump of sugar, gambolling playfully under your window and always on hand when you feel like going for a lovely ride. But the reality can be quite different from this rosy dream. Keeping a horse at home is a heavy responsibility: no matter what breed it is or for what you intend to use it. The horse always needs time, attention and daily care – not to mention such attentions as mucking out or those anxious nights when you have to wait up for the vet! Apart from needing a lot of space, a horse also needs to be exercised daily; if you leave it standing in the stable it can become dangerously ill with colic from lack of exercise. Finally, the companion you want to be happy will be bored and miserable if he is kept on his own. The gregarious nature of the horse, for centuries a herd animal, makes communication with other horses essential to its well being, deprived of this it can literally waste away. One often sees horses kept with other animals such as a sheep or even a hen, but nothing can take the place of its own kind. It is therefore essential to keep at least two horses, one of which may be a pony of course.

But these problems once accepted, what could be more wonderful than sharing the daily life of the noblest of domestic animals? Whether you have a thoroughbred ex-racehorse, an old school horse saved from being put down, a palomino – its coat flaming in the sunset – or a speedy, rough little pony, always ready to go off on a ride (sometimes the fun starts when you try to catch it!), horses bring so much happiness to their owner that the work entailed in keeping it is soon forgotten.

Some owners, totally bitten by the bug, even want to breed horses. A foal bred at home really does feel like a new member of the family.

Closeness, friendship, affection: keeping your own horse means all these things. But every day the routine of looking after your horse must be kept up: feeding, watering, taking care of the feet, grooming mane and tail, hair by hair ... A full time job!

# CHILDREN'S PONIES

A pony is more than just a child-sized horse. Young riders not only greatly develop their motive power thanks to the pony but they weave dreams around their friend. About the size of a large dog, and with a very independant character, reputed to be more intelligent than a horse, occasionally pig headed (the Shetland most notably so!), small ponies make wonderful companions. But be careful – a pony needs just as much care, attention and regular routine as a horse. Lacking this, your Shetland or Fjord pony can become as bad tempered and inclined to bite as he may be playful and loyal to the owner who treats him properly. Pony psychology, like that of the horse, is based upon the instinct of survival; he will go to a friend for protection and mistrust a capricious owner. But there are ponies and ponies. There may be a thousand more differences between the Shetland pony and the Connemara than exist between the same Connemara and a thoroughbred. In fact the distinction between horse and pony is entirely arbitrary and is based purely on size: 14.2 hands and over and it is called a horse, below 14.2 it is a pony. This is why the schooling and riding of larger ponies, particulary in the U.K. and to an increasing extent elsewhere, is on the lines of classical equitation. Of the twenty main breeds some are more suitable for children than others, including for example the Welsh pony, the Fjord pony, the Dartmoor, the New Forest (some as much as 14 hands high, others less than 12 hands) and, of the larger ponies, the Haflinger. New breeds have appeared through cross breeding, including the French saddle horse used in equestrian events and, in the United States, the pony of the Americas, a cross between a Shetland and an Appaloosan, which has resulted in a wonderfully kind and fun horse.

In the lists of companion animals one must include the Falabella, who was born to be a pet. The "smallest horse in the world", only measuring 7.2 hands maximum, gets its name from the Argentine family who first bred it. The breed was started by crossing small thoroughbred ponies and Shetlands and then breeding from the smallest Falabellas to get the tiny size. Having retained the morphology of the thoroughbred, the Falabella cannot be ridden but is sometimes used for driving. Fragile and difficult to breed true it needs a great deal of care. A horse which arouses great emotion, it is highly valued.

8

12

15

9

16

10

14

13 The Pony of the Americas, (11.2-13.2 hands) is the result of crossing Shetlands and Appaloosans (1).

The Iceland Pony (average 13 hands) is very strongly built and able to cope with the problems of its native terrain.

The Shetland (under 10 hands) is the most common children's pony (4).

The French Saddle Pony (just 14.2 hands) is a new breed resulting from various sporting pony crosses (5).

The Connemara (12.2-14.2), is the only Irish breed of Pony (6, 7).

The Haflinger (14.2), an Austrian pony, always chestnut with a light mane and tail, makes an excellent driving pony.

The Mérens Pony (13.3-14 hands) is an ancient breed found in the mountains and high valleys of the Arièga River in France.

The New Forest Pony (13.2-14.2 hands) is an excellent riding pony (10, 14).

The Fjord Pony (13.2-14.2 hands) comes from Norway and makes a marvellous trekking pony (12).

The Falabella must measure under 8 hands and retain a Thoroughbred appearance (15). There have been many other attempts to breed miniature ponies (15.)

# THE ARAB HORSE

The pure bred Arab horse has in the past inspired fanatical passion to the extent of religious fervour, and is today revered in stud farms which are veritable temples to the breed. The Arab's intrinsic beauty and finesse, its mobile head and straight nose, eyes which look made up, and flaring nostrils, its elongated neck and tail carried high give it a natural elegance. It is the symbol of equine beauty even though some say it is too small (around 14.1 – 15.1 hands). Most importantly, its amazing genetic ability to transfer its characteristics to its descendants make it a prince among horses. All the great breeds, from the heavy Percheron to the English thoroughbred, have marked Arab qualities. The exact origins of the breed are unknown but its evolution is certainly linked to the specific conditions of life in which it was reared: in the semi desert regions of the Middle East where no horse could live without man's help. The nomads always lived side by side with their mounts. Proud of their horses, the Bedouin bred them for their beauty and intelligence and their qualities of resistance, whilst in the VIIth century the Muslim religion worked hard on improving the breed for purposes of conquest. The prophet Mahomet himself often referred to the horse, linking the quality of care given to it by the faithful to a religious practice. In fact, in their conquest of southern Europe the Arabs' light horses were an advantage against the heavy and heavily caparisoned horses of the enemy. Europeans learnt a lesson from this and began to use Arab horses to improve their own breeding lines.

The passion inspired by the pure bred Arab horse is better understood today. Still used constantly to improve other breeds the Arab horse is bred for three purposes: racing restricted to the breed; as a saddle horse (particularly for endurance riding, in which he excels) and thirdly the sheer pleasure of maintaining famous bloodlines. Many owners, particularly in the homeland of the Arab horse and in the United States and again in Poland, shelter rare

pearls in sumptuous studs. The King of Morocco, for instance, built his Bouznika stud at enormous cost simply in order to shelter these pure bred sons of the desert of an almost sacred breed.

The pure bred Arab is the archetypal horse, Small (around 15.2 hands), it has a small head with a wide, flat forehead, often with a slightly dished face, a long fine neck, clean legs and powerful quarters. Its high tail carriage and its wide nostrils make it instantly recognisable.

# RACEHORSES

# THE THOROUGHBRED — NOBLESSE OBLIGE

Since the beginning of history man has raced horses. The Greeks gloried in chariot racing in the Olympic games, where teams of two or four horses pulled their chariots; the Romans contributed the spice of betting to the sport. But although pure speed competitions have always existed, it was not until the 18th century in England that racing became structured into the great modern race meetings which thrill spectators and punters from the United States to Hong Kong. Though monetary gain is one motivation for the sport, the sight of Thoroughbreds thundering along "like the blood in their veins"; the splendid effort as they throw themselves wholeheartedly into the fight, could explain the great success of racing by itself. The select world of the Thoroughbred, personified as much by the elegantly dressed racegoer as by the astronomical money paid for the best yearlings in prestigious sales at Newmarket in England, Kleeneland in the U.S.A or Deauville in France, is also fascinating.

But racing is still, above all, an incomparable means of selecting the best animals for breeding. Thoroughbred racing was born on the racecourses of England, at the end of the 17th century, under the influence of Charles II, who loved to ride in races himself. The first purpose built racecourse was created at Newmarket, together with the first rules and regulations governing the sport and the first Thoroughbred horses. The development and great success of racing encouraged breeders to take breeding seriously and to cross only their best mares with the Thoroughbred Arab stallions just brought into the country. Three stallions, imported between 1691 and 1728, entered the history books: the Byerley Turk, the Darley Arabian and the Godolphin Arabian. The latter, originally presented to King Louis XVth of France by the Bey of Tunis, was being used as a Paris carriage horse when he was noticed and bought by an English enthusiast. The Godolphin Arabian was great grandsire to Eclipse, who became the most famous racehorse of all time: never beaten in his

lifetime. These legendary stallions, whose stud books opened in 1791, are the ancestors of all Thoroughbreds today. Exported throughout the world, progressively better fed and trained, the precocious Thoroughbred (whose career starts at the age of two and finishes at five) has turned into an incomparable athlete who sets the standard for today's great racing worldwide.

Flat racing is the great test of the Thoroughbred. A win in the Prix de l'Arc de Triomphe (3: Saumarez in 1990) means a place in the history books. Some Thoroughbreds like Allez France (9) have become legends, which partly explains the fabulous sums paid at bloodstock sales (5). Thoroughbreds are also bred in Moroccan studs (10). The start is critical (2 & 8) and can determine racing positions (1 & 7) and even the ultimate result.

# BORN TO RACE

A lthough it has been known for a long time as the "English" Thoroughbred the breed has in fact become quite cosmopolitan. The United States, France and Ireland in particular can pride themselves on winning bloodlines. But this king of racehorses is also bred in Malaysia and Venezuela, and 21,000 foals a year make Australia the second largest exporter of the Thoroughbred after the United States (51,000).

Similarly, the most prestigious races were for a long time exclusively English, with the famous Epsom Derby (first run in 1780), the Thousand Guineas and the Two Thousand Guineas at Newmarket, but American and French race-courses today offer some equally prestigious races. In the United States, where the first Thoroughbred bloodlines were introduced in the 18th century, such races as the Kentucky Derby, first run in 1867, assured continuing quality of breeding; the names of Secretariat and Nijinsky being engraved on the minds of followers of the turf on both sides of the Atlantic. In the same way such great horses as Allez France have made French breeding famous, as have such prestigious race meetings as those of Chantilly and Longchamps, home of the Prix de L'Arc de Triomphe.

However, despite their common ancestry, notable differences exist between different nations' bloodlines. The American Thoroughbred is an excellent sprinter, used to giving its all over short distances (1,000 to 1,450 metres), while European classic races tend to be run over 2,000 metres or, for certain long distance races, 4,000 metres. The qualities required to win on different sides of the Atlantic are therefore obviously different, which in turn affects the qualities looked for in breeding. Training methods vary too: while the Americans prefer short bursts of fast galloping, in Europe we like to train on long-distance training gallops at the canter, to work on the horse's wind and stamina. This is why, despite the superior numbers of American Thoroughbreds, they have not made more impact in Europe.

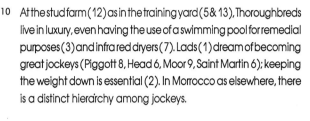

At the stud farm (12) as in the training yard (5 & 13), Thoroughbreds live in luxury, even having the use of a swimming pool for remedial purposes (3) and infra red dryers (7). Lads (1) dream of becoming great jockeys (Piggott 8, Head 6, Moor 9, Saint Martin 6); keeping the weight down is essential (2). In Morrocco as elsewhere, there is a distinct hierarchy among jockeys.

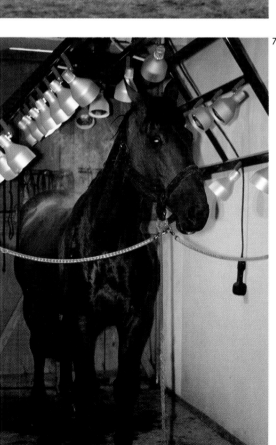

# STEEPLECHASING — THE SUPREME TEST

While flat racing may be the public's favourite test of the Thoroughbred, steeplechasing is undoubtedly the most impressive. This pitiless form of racing requires, as well as speed, tenacity, strength and an ability to jump, which turns Thoroughbreds into all round athletes. In fact Thoroughbreds are often trained as 'chasers when early training (which begins at the precocious of age of 18 months although full growth is not attained until the horse is 3 years old) shows that the horse is not quite fast enough for flat racing but is proving itself a good jumper. They follow a very different career and will take part in numerous hurdle races before qualifying for the classic steeplechase races (which require exceptional endurance: often being run over 5,000 or even 6,000 metres).

Steeplechasing was one of the first forms of racing between individuals; it gets its name from the fact that such races were run over fields, streams, hedges etc. between points marked by near or distant church steeples, in the great tradition of betting between hunting gentlemen. Racecourse jumps perpetuate this tradition and so may take the form of hedges, ditches or walls  Although the obstacles to be jumped may look impossibly high to the spectator they are nevertheless always jumpable, and appear imposing enough to the horse for him to make the necessary effort of his own accord, without slowing down, thereby minimising the risks.

The best known steeplechase is the redoubtable Grand National run over the Aintree course at Liverpool, which every year has its share of spectacular falls and has the whole of Britain holding its breath. Its most daunting obstacle is the famous Beecher's Brook, a water jump preceded by a 4 foot 10 inch high fence (3 foot 3 inches wide on top) on the take-off side and a 5 foot 6 inch wide natural brook on the landing side! Other prestigious steeplechases include the Cheltenham Gold Cup, the French Prix du Président de la République run at Auteuil, and the American Grand National.

10

Much more demanding for horse and jockey alike than flat racing, racing over hurdles and steeplechasing are open to older horses (3 & 6). A great natural jump is essential to get over sometimes frightening obstacles like the water at Auteuil (1). Katko (5, 10, 11) is a new tremendous jump. When jumping the jockey sits in to the horse, almost leaning back (9, 12).

7

12

8

9

11

# TROTTING HORSES, SUPERIORITY OF THE PART BRED

Nothing equals the feeling of sheer power given by trotting horses as they lunge forward under the impulsion of their hindquarters, body stretched out in supreme effort, nostrils dilated to catch oxygen, moving so fast they hardly touch the ground. The great trotting horses, and the jockeys who drive their sulkies, are real stars and the world of trotting, much less elitist than that of conventional horse racing, attracts a huge public.

The trot, unlike the gallop which is the crowning pace of the horse, is the most useful working pace. A horse cannot maintain a gallop over long distances as it is an assymetrical three beat pace with a fourth suspended beat, while the trot (a two beat diagonal pace in which each foreleg hits the ground in time with the diagonally opposite hind leg), is muscularly in balance and therefore less tiring on the horse. In the days of horse drawn transport, mailcoaches and private carriages used the trot to cover long distances as fast as possible. Trotting races were first run in the 18th century in the style of conventional races, in order to improve the breeding of half-bred horses. In 1777, one Count Orloff, a Russian, bred the first trotters intended for racing by repeatedly crossing Danish mares with English Thoroughbreds and pure bred Arabs. Known as the Orloff Trotter, this breed was to hold the title of world champion right up until the turn of the century. Similarly, mares of Norman origin and Thoroughbred stallions were the founders of the present French Trotting lines, who alone rival the great American trotting lines, despite the fact that some Northern European countries as well as Italy and New Zealand are also trotting enthusiasts. First bred in 1849, by crossing Thoroughbreds with English Hackney horses (traditionally used to pull the mail) and certain local breeds, the American Standardbred produced some incredible record breakers. The amazing Mack Lobel, beaten later by Ourasi in a race of the century, ran an incredible mile in 1 minute 52.2 seconds at Garden State Park.

Mounted trotting races are only run in France, where even sulky drivers ride. Experts see in this tradition, which develops strength and endurance in the horse, one of the reasons why the French are so successful in breeding Trotters for driving races.

Driven trotting races take a great deal of effort (6 & 1). Ridden trotting races (3, 4, 5, 8) are best known in France, but Scandinavian horses (11, 14) and above all American standardbreds (15) make fantastic trotters. The legendary Ourasi (13) won the top American Grand Prix four times.

# MORE HORSES FOR COURSES

The Thoroughbred and the Trotting Horse do not have the exclusive right to the racecourse. One of the most famous races for other breeds is the All-American Futurity for Quarter Horses. The Quarter Horse, descended from crosses between the Mustang and the Thoroughbred, gets its name from the fact that it runs best over a distance of a quarter mile. Sprint races, which exist only in North America, are very popular in that country. The whole breed, constantly improved by careful selection for breeding, does well: this small horse with incredibly fast take off is sought after also for its agility and skill in cutting out cattle and is the most popular breed in the United States.

Another American speciality is the Walking Horse, which uses a gait which in Europe is considered to be a false gait. It is in fact a lateral trot (in which the legs are synchronised on the same side rather than diagonally) and is extremely comfortable for the rider. Some Standardbreds are trained (in fact constrained) to practice this gait from the earliest age. Harnessed to a sulky, like their trotting colleagues, they are extremely fast: their record for the mile is 1 minute 52 seconds as against 1 minute 54.2 seconds for Trotting Horses.

Racing pure-bred Arab horses is, in both Europe and the United States, strongly regaining popularity at the moment. Although nowhere near as fast as the Thoroughbred, Arabs race against each other in all corners of the globe, (including Turkey and what used to be the U.S.S.R.). Some Western breeders hope that in popularising Arab racing they will introduce into the breed athletic qualities for which it will be sought as well as purely aesthetic ones. The same concerns for the breed explain the fact that Anglo-Arab racing is still practiced in southern France. The Anglo-Arab is of course a cross between the pure bred Arab and the English thoroughbred; fine blood horses, they are mostly bred for equestrian sports.

Extremely partial to racing, the ex-Soviet countries, who have a very small breeding programme (barely 300 foals a year) put their money on the Russian Tersky. A descendant of the pure bred Arab mixed with the Thoroughbred, these very elegant horses race on the flat against pure bred Arabs, which are extremely popular.

Sprint races are king in the United States (2, 4, 12) in which Quarter Horses run (5) incredible times. Standardbreds (7, 10) also compete in the specialist American walking races (13). The Tersky (11), the Anglo-Arab, and pure bred Arabs (6, 9) race throughout the world.

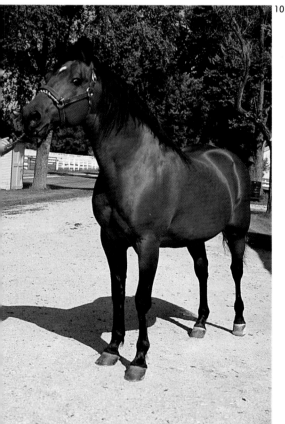

# DRESSAGE AND DRIVING HORSES

# EQUITATION AS AN ART

Like all the finest Western traditions, classical equitation first saw the light of day in Renaissance Italy, where Pignatelli, Grisone and Fiaschi choreographed truly dancing figures out of the sophisticated movements used by horses on the battlefield. Aesthetically inspiring, equitation became an art which was taken up by the courts of Europe, still linked to the techniques used in war. And so developed the haute école figures, from the Spanish gait (a pace of incredible nobility, in which the horse moves forward throwing its forelegs out straight in front) which was used to split the enemy lines, to the most complex of airs, the *capriole* (a leap into the air in which all 4 legs leave the ground simultaneously), which originally allowed the rider to escape when surrounded. Freed from its military origins, the aim of the art of haute école was to attain a high level of dressage which was based on the horse's natural paces and abilities, denuded of artifice, and which cultivated natural movement even in the airs above the ground: the *croupade,* for instance, corresponds to the natural kicking out of a horse and the *capriole* to the leap of a foal. France quickly became the home of equitation, with masters such as Francois Robichon de la Guérinière (1687-1751), who is considered to be the father of classical equitation as we know it today. He taught above all the value of training "light", that is to say without artificial constraints. The Saumur Academy Cadre Noir continues to perpetuate the tradition of the great 19th century masters such as Aure, Baucher and l'Hotte, whose works are the bible of the finest exponents of horsemanship. Paradoxically it is at the Spanish Riding School of Vienna that the French style of equitation is most closely followed today; there the masters still train the famous Lippizzaners on the principals of La Guérinière, their matching grey coats adding to the unforgettable uniformity of their performance. The Lippizzaners get their name from the Lippizza Stud, today located in Yugoslavia, where the Archduke Charles of Austria founded the breed in the 16th century, breeding from Andalusians. The Andalusian indeed seems born to haute école work. Originally used as a war horse, the breed is descended from crosses between Spanish mares and pure bred Arabs.

Intelligence and a high stepping gait are characteristic of the breed. The ancient monastery of Jerez in Spain, although less well known than the school of Vienna, also maintains the classical tradition. In Portugal one individual trainer, Nonu Oliveira, considered to be the master of modern times, taught enthusiasts from all over the world until his death in 1989. The tradition has since been carried on by his son.

The Spanish Riding School of Vienna (1, 4, 5, 10) is the most famous riding academy in the world, with its celebrated Lippizzaners (6), their incomparable skill demonstrated here by a *pesade* in hand (11). The Saumur Academy Cadre Noir (7) carries on the high school tradition, here perforoming a *croupade* (13) and a *courbette* (12). In Portugal, Nuno Oliveira was the greatest classical trainer of modern times and the Portuguese Academy (2) competes with that of Jerez in Spain (3, 9).

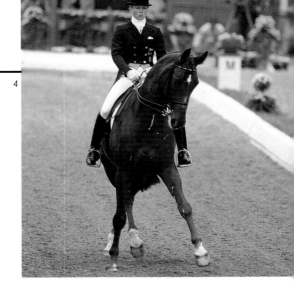

# DRESSAGE, THE TEST OF A HORSE'S TRAINING

**W**ithout dressage there would be no equitation. Every rider, even one who wants to specialise in jumping, has to learn to master the aids correctly (legs, hands and seat) for his horse to go calmly and collectedly for him. These qualities, necessary to basic riding, are essential at the highest level of dressage competition. Dressage is, however, the poor relation in equestrian sports, even though it is a required Olympic discipline, probably because there is not as much public understanding and enthusiasm for what is after all a very specialised subject – one much less easy for the uninitiated to understand and evaluate than the more obvious jumping competitions.

First held at the turn of the century, dressage competitions take place in rectangular dressage arenas (60 x 20 metres). The competitor performs a compulsory set of movements and judges (rather as in skating competitions) give points for perfection of individual movements and a number of general impressions such as lightness, impulsion and correct use of the aids. Tests are classified partly by degree of difficulty of the required movements and partly by degree of training and attitude of the horse. The simplest dressage tests require a calm horse who proves himself capable of carrying out simple exercises in a collected, forward-going manner (rein back, halt, change of rein at all three paces). Olympic standard tests are incomparably more complex, requiring a mastery of high school movements (known as airs). Though they are not asked to perform any leaps (such as a *capriole*), the horse and rider do have successfully to perform such movements as the *passage* (a kind of slow trot with a very high action (the horse appearing to move more upward than forward), the *piaffe* (trotting on the spot, without moving forward) and changes of leg (changing from a canter where the horse is striking off with the left foot to a canter where it is striking off with the right without stopping or slowing in between). The great difficulty, even more than achieving the movements, is to present the horse looking calm, foward going and right and totally dropping his head to the rider's hand (that is with a relaxed mouth). This level of dressage takes exceptional concentration and several years of hard work which rely as much on love as mastery.

Apart from the World Dressage Championships and Olympic games there is now also the dressage World Cup, where competitors give free style dressage performances to music, designing their own test and choosing their own music. Horses, sensitive to rhythm, soon pick up the idea of moving to music and the result is delightful to watch.

7

10

11

14

12

Dressage competition is dominated by the Germans. Reiner Klimke and his Westphalian Alherich (12), Margot Otto-Crepin and her Holstein Corlandus (9), Nicole Uphoff and Rembrandt (10) lead the world. World Cup Dressage tests to music are performed indoors and Robert Dover, sponsored by Federleicht (13 ) is often among the winners. Among the most spectacular movements are the *pirouette* (7, 13), a kind of half turn on the spot at the canter, the *half pass* (3, 4) where the horse moves sideways by crossing his front legs, and the *piaffe* (14). Dressage tests for ponies (1, 6) are the best training of all for adult competition.

8

9

13

# DRIVING, REMOTE CONTROL

**B**ringing back carriages which were fashionable in the 19th century (or, failing the real thing, faithful imitations), and using them for fun is an idea which appeals to many. Followers of the sport of driving, fascinated both by the wheeled vehicle and horses which respond to the "remote control" of voice and rein, are increasing. In the country and on the competition track top drivers accomplish real feats of skill, delighting the spectator. A fascinating and nostalgic performance – what could be more lovely than the sight of a pair of shining bay horses pulling a black derby brake with gleaming lamps?

Competitions, divided into classes by the number of horses driven (single, pair or, for the supreme test, four in hand) cover three tests: presentation and dressage, obstacle driving (overcoming winding and narrow obstacles) and a marathon. The latter is a kind of cross country test against the clock which requires specially adapted carriages (with disc brakes!), the climax of the fun being going through the water in a sparkling shower, which never fails to cause great excitement among the spectators.

Hungary and Holland in particular (thanks to Ysbrand Chardon and Ad Aarts, current world champion with the great bay horses which are as supple as they are generous in their movement) dominate competitive driving. The Dutch Friesian horse, black in colour with a high head carriage and long feathers, is also much favoured by drivers, as are Hungarian and Polish horses, these countries never having lost the tradition of driving as a sport. While some lovers of the art of driving content themselves with driving any large horse, certain breeds are particularly suited to the sport – such as the British Cleveland Bay and the Hackney, which is famous for its very high knee action, the Lippizzaner (Yugoslavian trainers from the Lippizza stud work them harnessed as well as ridden) and the American Morgan horse, whose courage is without rival. Pony driving, with specially built carriages, is also much in vogue, using the smallest to the biggest, from Shetlands, Haflingers and Welsh cobs to the big Landais bays.

9

12

14

10

Driving competitions are divided into 3 sections: presentation and dressage (11, 14), obstacle driving (10, 15) and a marathon (1, 3); a sometimes very difficult cross country phase (11), the highlight of which is going through the water (13). The grooms play an important part in this section in balancing the vehicle (8).

Competitions are for single horses, pairs – side by side or tandem – (6) or four in hand, the last being the most difficult to manage as it entails a series of reins which are complex to manipulate (12). Some breeds of horses have always been used as carriage horses, such as hackneys (2), with their spectacular action. But modern competition is dominated by the great Dutch horses (1). Pony driving trials are also very popular and make a good introduction to the sport. Haflingers in particular make excellent driving horses (14). The collar used in European driving is finer than that used for waggon racing (5), much in vogue in the United States.

13

11

15

# SHOWJUMPERS
# AND EVENTERS

# SHOWJUMPING — A BREATHTAKING SPORT

**B**alance, strength and speed are not enough. A showjumper must ally suppleness and dexterity to a true partnership with his rider. High level jumping competitions of all kinds are justly popular: the suspense they create and the qualities required to compete in them make jumping the star of equestrian sports. From cross country competition (where the clock rules) to puissance events (where the horse that can jump the highest wins) there are numerous jumping competitions, but most are based on simple rules: the competitor has to take a number of obstacles in a pre-ordained sequence; if their mount knocks down a pole or puts a foot in the water (the only long jump on a showjumping course) it is penalised 4 points. The first refusal or run out (when the horse stops or avoids the jump at the last minute) only receives a 3 point penalty, but a second incurs six points and a third means elimination from the competition. Victory goes to the horse and rider with the least number of penalty points (the ideal being a clear round). Equal scorers go on to one or more further rounds in which the jumps are raised and/ or riders compete against the clock and the fastest equal score wins. Speed is essential, suspense and showmanship are paramount, and the public love it. The height of the jumps is not the greatest difficulty, in international competition horses jump as high as 1.70m (5 feet, 5 inches) and the world record, held by the Chilean Captain Morales and Huaso since 1949, is 2.47m (8 feet).

The real difficulty is in getting round an extremely tight course, which necessitates having to cut corners at speed without being out of balance to meet the next jump right. Knowledgeably designed by an expert, a jumping course may be full of traps. The horse's training is of course of paramount importance.

Since jumping competitions began, at the end of the 19th century, courses have become more and more complex and techniques more and more refined. But it was only in 1912, following in the footsteps of the Italian master Caprilli, and the style of American jump jockeys, that Colonel Danloux brought the modern method of jumping, with the seat raised out of the saddle and the balance forward, into general use – up until then everyone jumped seat firmly down and leaning back, which tended to unbalance both horse and rider. Danloux's method of leaning forward so as to preserve the horse and rider's natural centre of gravity allowed the horse freedom of movement and was the starting point of modern jumping.

Taking a jump is made up of three stages: the approach (5, 9), the take off (15) and the landing (18). The horse must lift its forehand well off the ground (13) and have very powerful quarters (14) as well as staying balanced throughout the course (3). The biggest problem is when the rider loses his own balance (16)!

While indoor winter competitions (6) are increasing in number only big outdoor courses can give a real variety of jumps: apart from the many oxers (4, 8) and uprights (11) there are many other kinds of obstacle, including water jumps (1), banks (7), gates (12), walls with poles (10), or without (2). Walls are also used for puissance competitions (17).

# THE GREAT COMPETITIONS AND NATIONS

**A**ll great horsemen dream of victory in an Olympic games, the supreme test. The World championships, which also run every four years (but two years apart from the games so as not to clash) also mean the discipline of long training for international teams. Between these two competitions come the Nations' Cups. Each country in the International Equestrian Federation may organise one Nations' Cup a year within CSIO (Concours de Saut International Officiel) rules. These competitions are extremely popular with public and riders alike. In the winter, showjumpers (who once had a hard-earned rest at this time of year) now jump in indoor competition on the World Cup circuit whose final is held in a different city every year.

The history of the CSIO, confined to military riders up until the 1950s, is dotted with the great names of showjumping of all nationalities, including women (notably the Americans Melanie Smith and Katherine Burdsall), who were first allowed to ride against men in this competition. Paradoxically, while showjumping was invented by the Irish and the English there are few British Olympic medals: no Briton has ever won an individual gold and a British team has only won the team gold once, in 1952. An irony of fate, since British riders such as David Broome (world champion in 1970) and the Whittaker brothers are amongst the greatest riders in the world. But they faced stiff competition: from the Germans (Winkler and Schockemohle), the Italians (D'Inzeo, king in the 1960s, and Mancinelli), the Americans (Steinkraus, the first great American horseman, and Jo Fargis) and the French (including Jean Paul d'Oriola, the first rider to win two Olympic golds, in Helsinki in 1952 and Mexico in 1964).

The horses too are legend, well loved showjumpers of all nationalities have become household names and the great rivalry between two of them, John Whittaker's Milton and Pierre Durand's Jappeloup (both small, enchantingly courageous animals who sailed over jumps far bigger than themselves) kept the showjumping world holding its breath for years, only coming to àn end with the death from natural causes of Jappeloup in 1991.

Famous showjumpers who take part In the Olympics (8) receive a lot of publicity. The 1980s were the years of the duel between the British Milton (9, 10), John Whittaker's great showjumper, and the French Jappeloup (1, 2) ridden by Pierre Durand. Germany's Paul Schockemohle and Deister (7), America's Joe Fargis and his thoroughbred A Touch of Class (11) are also at the top in showjumping. Malcolm Pyrah (3) and the Brasilian Nelson Pessoa have been top of the bill for two or three decades. Also shown here are the American Kursinsky (4), the Swiss Fuchs (6) and the Frenchman Navet with his stallion Quito de Baussy (5).

Some competitions in order to draw the crowds take place in fun settings like that of Arcachon, which takes place on a beach (13), And the horses get their rewards too (12)!

# BRED TO JUMP

The ideal showjumper has short, powerful quarters, clean legs with solid hocks and a straight, unhollowed back: temperamentally the horse needs to be courageous and calm, the latter a limiting factor in the use of thoroughbreds, which often tend to hot up. The Americans, however, who do not have any indigenous breed that will take them to the top in jumping, use them successfully.

The popularity of show jumping has led to careful breeding in many European countries in the attempt to produce half bred horses suitable for the sport. Irish and British hunters make the best showjumpers in the world, but Germany and France are beginning to catch up. Trakheners (amongst them the celebrated stallion Abdullah, a long-term member of the American national team) and German Holsteins are incomparably powerful and willing to have a go at anything. On the other hand they sometimes lack the lightness over the ground of, for example, the Anglo-Arab, (the result of crossing English Thoroughbreds and pure bred Arabs). For some years Dutch and Belgian horses (sometimes with French or German blood) have figured in the list of champions. The ex-Soviets use such breeds as the Budyonny and the Akhal Teke, with its amazing silvery-striped coat reminiscent of a greyhound in pattern. These indigenous breeds are capable of competing with the best in the world, and with the ending of the cold war are likely to be seen more often in Europe.

Ponies are naturally good jumpers and perhaps better developed for the sport than full size horses (thanks to the comparative strength of their quarters). Competitions for ponies are divided into four categories by size: Grade A (wherein Shetlands are very successful), up to grade D (for ponies up to 14 hands). International competition is limited to the latter. While many breeds, including new Forest, Welsh and Haflinger ponies take part in these competitions, it is the Connemara (descended in part from the Thoroughbred) that is the most successful. It was a Connemara, called Dundrum, that won the silver medal in the 1968 Olympic games in Mexico.

Certain European breeds of horse are always among the competitors at big shows: the Trakheners whose star is the stallion Abdullah (10), the Hanoverians (2), Irish horses like Mill Pearl (11), French saddle horses like Flambeau (5) and Anglo Arabs like Jiva (4). But sometimes unknowns can be a surprise entry, like the American Nepomuk (14). Horses from the East such as the Akhal Teke (1) will doubtless play a bigger role in the future.

In the pony classes Shetlands (13) compete as fiercely as the bigger ponies which are almost the size of horses. Among these the New Forest pony (9) and the French Saddle pony (9) have trouble beating the Connemara (12), it's not all plain sailing (3) but the prizes are worth it (7)!

# EVENTING

An exciting spectator sport (particularly the cross country phase, which is the heart of one or three day eventing) where the jumps are made up of solid tree trunks, stone walls, roadways, timber combinations, water jumps, steps, etc., asking everything of the horse and rider – who need nerves of steel – eventing is a test of all the horse's skills: speed, jumping ability and dressage. In a three day event the first day is a dressage test, the third a showjumping competition to close the event and the second is devoted to the most difficult part: the cross country phase. The latter is over a course which is in itself divided into sections. In top class international eventing, the first part of the cross country is a fast ride over some 4 miles, followed by a steeplechase section (the problems of timekeeping mean covering this at the gallop); and a second phase of open country some 4-8 miles long, preceding a final cross country section over horrendous solid obstacles, which to the eye of a man on the ground look quite impossible to jump. Reaching the end of the course does not necessarily mean finishing either; any lame or exhausted horse which does not pass the veterinary examination which follows will be eliminated. In order to win it is necessary to be up among the leaders on each of the three days; a bad result in the dressage or showjumping sections can be as fatal as a slow cross country round.

Originally limited to military riders, eventing has often been criticised as being too rough on the horse and too dangerous. But apart from the fact that horses, aware of the solidity of cross country jumps, tend to jump very clear of them, accidents are no more frequent than in other equestrian disciplines. It is wonderful to see top class horses competing at the height of physical fitness and achievement after long months of rigorous preparatory training for an event.

Different levels of eventing exist, of course, for more or less experienced riders and horses: competitions for novices (already hardened horsemen!) or young horses are much less severe, both as to jumps and distance as well as time limit. The same goes for eventing for ponies – who make ideal mounts for learning the difficulties of cross country, being courageous and forward going. They can teach a young rider the excitement of speed without fear of a fall. And they develop the qualities of a real horseman able to overcome any imaginable problem.

Three day eventing is divided into 3 tests: dressage (9), showjumping (13) and cross country. This last is in turn divided into roads and fields (4), a steeplechase section (6) and a cross country section, which includes dizzily high or difficult fences (16) which require as much nerve as drive and determination (1, 5, 7, 12, 17). Any kind of jump is allowed provided it is a fixed obstacle. Water jumps (2, 14, 15) and staggered drop jumps (10) are highlights of the course.

# THE BRITISH LEAD

The names of Badminton and Burghley ring in the ears of all lovers of eventing as does Indianapolis in the ears of motor racing enthusiasts. These two annual British competitions are the most exciting, difficult and therefore prestigious competitions in eventing. Only the Olympic games rank higher. Eventing is extremely popular in Britain, much more so than in other countries, and thousands of spectators every year take their picnics to the cross country course at Badminton. Some years the presence of Princess Anne also heightens public interest in eventing. The presence of successful women riders on the winners' podium is one of the characteristics of modern day eventing and proves that courage is not the prerogative of men alone. Lucinda Greene, world champion in 1982, and Virginia Leng who followed her in 1986, have demonstrated how much eventing can be a woman's sport.

Anglo-Saxons shamelessly dominate the international scene in eventing, be they New Zealanders (like Mark Todd and Charisma, gold medallists in 1984), English (Ian Stark for example) or, to a lesser degree, Americans and Australians. Although German riders have given us the odd surprise in recent years, it is noticeable that they have done so on English horses. It is English mounts, often close to Thoroughbreds, more than the riders even, which make the difference. Eventing requires the horse to be a true athlete with absolute confidence in the rider (and vice versa!), with courage, endurance and undaunting tenacity, allied to the ability to get round at great speed.

Badminton (16, 13) attracts thousands of spectators every year. Mounted judges (15) are part of the tradition. Among the great champions Mark Todd (5 & 6) and Ian Stark (1, 14) have both won Badminton. Many British riders are at the top level of eventing, such as Mark Phillips (7) and also German riders such as Erhorn (3), Spaniards like Golding (11), French, Touzaint (12) and the Polish rider I. Piasecki (2). Ponies too take novice riders round frightening jumps (8, 10), provided they get through a dressage test (9) and a showjumping section first.

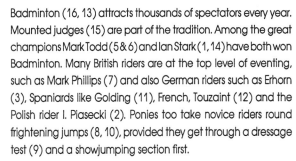

# THE GREAT OUTDOORS

# THE COUNTRYSIDE ON HORSEBACK

**R**iding out (known as "hacking out" to horsemen) gives one a completely new view of the world. Far from the noise and bustle of towns and machinery, any pony or horse may take its rider into the heart of the forest and introduce them to a new and secret world. Silence takes on a new quality when the only sound is that of regular and smooth hoof beats, which do not frighten off other animals, as would a human footstep. The forest welcomes horse and rider as though they belonged there – down a side track a deer may suddenly appear and bound serenely away or further on a squirrel may be nibbling a nut and barely taking any notice of the curious cavalcade approaching under his vault of greenery. And the pleasure of galloping along an endless beach, in the sea breeze, is indescribable.

In some European countries riding out was for a long time treated only as something that gave the horse a little relaxation between schooling sessions, but even there it is becoming appreciated as an important part of equestrian practice. In Britain, the U.S.A., Australasia and other countries, of course, it has always been regarded as an important, indeed essential, part of equestrian life (if not the ultimate goal of learning to ride). When riding, in the sixties, ceased to be available only to a privileged few, many nature lovers took to the horse as a means both of conquering the great outdoors and of getting to know an animal which has always been man's servant. Not getting much fun from the dust of a manege such people from their very first lesson are eager to learn to stay in the saddle over all kinds of country. The Western saddle, which gives more security to the beginner than the traditional English saddle, which is flatter and not as easy to stick on in an emergency, can be a great help here. The development of equestrian tourism quickly followed: riding holidays and horse drawn caravan holidays attracted the new horsemen. In groups they took off for one day or longer trips of exploration, led by professionals who were in charge and responsible for planning and the care of man and horse alike. Numerous organisations offer such riding holidays whose cheap cost, when compared with a winter sports holiday for instance, is often not realised. You may wander Ireland in a horse drawn caravan or discover the fairytale byways of Cappadocia on some small but sturdy Turkish horse. Many tourists confined to the heat of their motor cars would be envious of this privileged way of seeing a country – if they only but knew what they were missing!

Pony or horse trekking give the word freedom its true meaning – as you sit up above the world in a silence that permeates from the tip of your riding boot to the top of your hard hat.

9

8

10

11

Freedom, the wide open spaces and communion with nature: the countryside looks quite different from the back of a horse. In the Camargue (1), on the beaches of the North Sea (5), at Mont Saint Michel (3), in Bermuda (12), in Andalusia (6, 9) or Portugal (8, 12), in the Alps (14), on the banks of the Yonne in France (13), or simply in any field or forest, trekking on horseback opens the doors to a dream world.

12

14

13

# COMPANIONS IN FREEDOM

Now that the horse is once again free in the wide open spaces for too long left to the "iron horse", ever increasing numbers of trekking and trail riding groups and clubs are being organised. It is with these that trekking competitions began, now crowned by a European Championship in which placings take into account horse management skills (for example the rider has to be able to replace a damaged shoe himself and apply basic veterinary first aid) and those of the trekker (a map and compass – and the skill to use them – are all that is required here).

Such competitions are not as popular as straightforward trekking. However, great rallies of trekking enthusiasts are common and make wonderfully spectacular events for enthusiasts. Groups form in different corners of a region, or even a country, and arrange a precise meeting point at which they are to rally, and rallies culminate in a great equestrian party. One of the most famous of these is the internationally renowned *Route du Sel* (meaning saddle road) which has taken place with great success for some years now in the French Midi. On these historic rallies, with their friendly atmosphere, any enthusiast can join the great caravan of riders: mounted on a donkey, at the reins of a driving turn out, on a Shetland pony, a Barbary horse (the small sturdy North African breed whose qualities of endurance and adaptability to the countryside make them ideal trekking horses) or on one of the American breeds which are particularly well suited to long distance riding, such as the Appaloosan or the Palomino. Here there are no rosettes awarded – the only winner is the one who enjoys himself most. Such long distance rallies exist throughout the world, from Mongolia to Southern Morocco, where the "Horsemen of the Desert" rally every year. Some riders prefer to go off on their own, or with just one partner, on long distance rides which are real adventures. After months of hard preparation they may decide to cross America from north to south or, as was accomplished in 1973 by two pioneers of long distance riding, the Coquet sisters, follow in the steps of one Godefroi de Bouillon – who rode all the way from Paris to Jerusalem – a historic if slightly mad accomplishment. But despite the difficulties of adventure and the discomforts it entails, few are the "great travellers" who decide to put their feet on the ground for good.

On the back of a horse or in a horse drawn caravan, crossing some great American desert or steep mountain chain, the horse is an invitation to adventure. (1, 2, 3, 4, 5, 6, 7, 10, 11, 12, 14, 15).

The famous Route du Sel (Saddle road) rally in France, like other great rallies organised in other countries, brings together hundreds of enthusiasts every year following in the footsteps of history (8, 9, 13).

# ENDURANCE RIDING — THE SUPREME EFFORT

A hundred miles a day, averaging between 7 and 10 miles an hour, depending on the difficulties of the course, attempting to get there, not just first but with your horse in the best possible condition: these are the aims of endurance riding. A magnificent equestrian discipline in which the horse is tested to the limit of its endurance, in which the rider must judge precisely his horse's capabilities (and is often seen running alongside the horse at certain stages to rest it) and wherein the tactics used in getting through are of the first importance. Endurance competitions have existed in fact for a long time: back in the 19th century military riders competed over long distance courses and in the United States the exploits of the Pony Express are still legendary. It is on such experiences that the rules of endurance riding are based.

To obviate the accidents of the past, competitions today are strictly controlled: competing horses undergo frequent veterinary checks during the course of the competition – any suggestion of lameness or the slightest hint of cardiac weakness will mean instant elimination – and they are checked again when they have completed the course. Novice long distance riders learn to judge their horses' capabilities and needs over much shorter courses (first 18 and then 36 miles). Seventy-five-mile-a-day competitions are only for rigorously trained and experienced horses and riders, and the top distance of 100 miles is achieved only by the best in this field. Long distance or endurance riding has been popular in the United States for many years (the most famous endurance competition in the world is the Tevis Cup, held over a redoubtable and tricky California course, in which hundreds of riders compete) and in Australia (where the Quilty Cup is legendary) and it has a growing following in the U.K. and Europe.

The choice of long distance mount is based on a number of criteria: of course the horse must have healthy feet and be sure footed, with a rhythmic and slow heartbeat and even breathing to sustain ongoing effort. He must also have a proven and independant temperament (never being allowed to follow the lead of other competitors!). Many native ponies and horses as well as Barbarys and Appaloosans make perfectly good endurance horses, but best of all is the pure bred Arab, as evidenced by the World Champion Grand Sultan, who, with Becky Hart of the United States, showed himself to be an incredible glutton for mileage and of whom his fellow competitors only ever glimpsed the rear end.

11 Endurance riding is the art of fast, long distance riding: you must know the route like the back of your hand (3), take great care of the horse and have good back up, be able for example to replace a shoe (5). American breeds (2, 6), Arabs and Barbary horses (15) make great endurance horses. But sometimes horses of mixed blood do well too. Mao IV (8, 12) proved to be the best endurance horse in Europe, having learnt his job in a trekking centre!

# HUNTING

**Y**ou could almost say that it all began with hunting. Together with military riding, hunting is the origin of most kinds of equestrian sport, from racing (steeplechasing) to showjumping. Man has hunted throughout history and since time immemorial worked with his faithful companions, horse and hound. It was the nobles of the Renaissance who laid down the rules of the chase and turned it into a true sport, the spirit of which was not to be transgressed. There is an art to hunting, and the huntsman is as much a craftsman as is a boatswain, to take another example of a sporting leader. The huntsman, from the top of his horse, also plays the indispensable role of director or referee.

Huntsmen need to be keen on dogs and they also need to be exceptional horsemen, as do those who ride in the field. Following the hunt across a difficult country is no joke, particularly in Ireland and England, where fox hunting is a great tradition. Following the hunt here is true sport, entailing getting over jumps of all kinds and heights: walls, ditches and other obstacles which are terrifying enough to frighten a champion. Great Irish and English hunters have always been bred for the sport. Over flat, galloping country more thoroughbred horses are hunted and over uneven or difficult terrain the sure footed country breeds, a native pony, or a part bred hunter (part Irish perhaps) come into their own. In the U.S.A, American Saddle Horses are often used for hunting.

England and Ireland have the best hunting in the world (1, 2, 9). The fox is hunted here as it was in the last century and excellent horsemanship is needed to follow a field. In France deer and hare are hunted, and the huntsman wears a sword (12). Hounds which live and hunt in packs (6) are the real heroes of the chase. While many people may have a day's hunting by invitation (13) it is difficult to become a hunt member (4, 7).

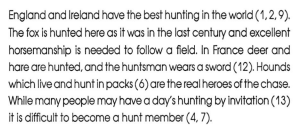

# GAMES ON HORSEBACK

# POLO, THE KING OF SPORTS

**P**olo, the king of sports, is the most ancient in the world, being invented some 2,000 years ago in Persia, from which country it spread throughout the Asian continent. The British first played Polo in India in the 19th century, where the small Manipuri pony (which rarely stood more than 13 hands high) was particularly suited to the game, being so agile. Cavalry officers and tea planters became very enthusiastic about polo and they first brought it to England in 1859. The British laid down the strict rules of the game, rendered necessary by the risks of collision, which are still in force today. It is against the rules for instance to cut in front of an opponent or zig zag in his path (under pain of being penalised by the two mounted referees). Two teams, of 4 players each, play against each other on a huge field (from 250 to 300 yards long and 160 – with side boards – to 200 yards wide). As in most ball games, the aim is to score a goal by hitting the ball into the opponents goal, in this case using a kind of mallet known as a polo stick. A handicapping system avoids unbalanced matches. Each player gains a personal handicap (from 0 up to 10 for the great players) and teams declare their total handicap (if a weaker team finds itself facing a stronger one in a tournament, it benefits from a goal advantage equal to the difference in handicaps). A match consists of five or eight seven-and-a-half-minute periods (a chukka). Even these short periods exhaust the pony, which must be changed every chukka, and therefore each player needs to bring a minimum of two ponies to a match. Polo is in fact a very demanding game for the horse, which has to make instant turns or take off at speed at the lightest signal. Argentinian ponies have dominated the international polo scene for decades: bred from the local criollo horses crossed with thoroughbreds, they have exceptional qualities of manoeuvrability, speed and an instinct for the game. Polo ponies are bred for the game in Argentina as nowhere else – and polo attracts football-sized crowds there. Polo, considered to be a select and expensive sport,

9

12

13

6

10

remains, unfortunately, for the few, although it has been more widely developed in the United States and in England, where Prince Charles, an excellent player, draws the crowds. But the numbers of players worldwide are growing and the future looks happy for a sport which requires, skill, excellent reflexes, physical strength and horsemanship.

7

11

Learning to play polo takes a long time. You have to master the straight shot, forward or backward from a swing (2) which may in turn be forward or backhand (3) and the swing must be carried through after hitting the ball. Because of the risk of being hit, horses and riders wear protective gear: boots (12) and tail protectors for the former and knee pads and helmets for the latter, who always wear white breeches and brown boots. Like golf clubs, polo sticks have different heads (13). The descendants of Argentine Criollos (4) make the best polo ponies.

8

14

# PADDOCK POLO AND GYMKHANA GAMES

To play polo costs a lot of money, and finding sites with enough open land to form a polo ground is difficult, and these two factors have led to the invention of "paddock polo" which is played to the same rules and principles but scaled down. The ball, which is larger, is made of rubber (instead of willow or bamboo) and the teams limited to three players each. The distances to be covered, considerably less than in the full-scale game, are less fatiguing for the horses and, paradoxically, almost more spectacular, as the players are evenly matched. Junior polo for children is played on an even smaller ground, being in proportion to the size of the children's ponies, and can be tiny – for Shetland ponies, for example.

Many other games encourage a healthy competitive spirit among clients at riding schools, allowing them to enjoy themselves while improving their technique of sticking in the saddle, and becoming independent of rein and stirrup, without having to rely on the boring old exercises of the schooling ring. Among such games are ones that recall the jousts of the Middle Ages (where competitors, riding at full gallop, tilted at golden rings with the ends of their lances, or offered hard-won bouquets to their chosen lady).

Gymkhanas have produced a spate of imaginative games on horseback for children: relay races or individual competitions such as the rose game, where three competitors try to grab the rose carried in a third's buttonhole, or push ball, where the ponies push a huge balloon with their chests towards the opposing goal, or the favourite equestrian version of musical chairs, where each time the music stops the rider has to jump down and sit on one of the bales of straw round which the ponies circle, and of which there is always one fewer than the number of competitors. The rider left standing is out. There is no limit to the number of equestrian games the imagination can devise: there are thousands of ways of playing games on horseback and they are all as beneficial to the horses (who throw themselves into the spirit of the fun, happy to get away from routine work) as they are to the rider.

10

6

11

7

12

Some of the many gymkhana games (1) include tilting at rings (13), orange sticking (12) and relay racing (11). New games only take a little imagination to invent (8, 14). Paddock polo (5, 10) brings polo within the reach of everyone.

8

14

9

13

# HORSE BALL

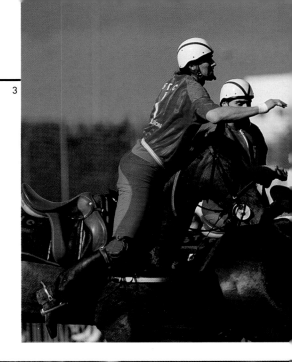

The latest equestrian sport and one which is both absorbing to play and exciting to watch is horse ball. Invented in France in the 1970s, it is gradually becoming more international and is played in most European countries today.

The invention of horse ball was made possible by the overcoming of two apparently impossible difficulties: how to get a grip on a round ball from the top of a horse and how actually to reach down to the ground and still be able to pull oneself back in the saddle (and without all the tack going, too). The first was solved by ringing the leather ball with eight large handles which are easily grasped, and the second by running a loose girth under the horse, from stirrup to stirrup, so that the rider, leaning right down to the ground to pick up the ball, could pull himself back in the saddle simply by exerting pressure with his outside leg. At a stroke the classic problem of all ball games on horseback was solved and a game was invented which combines the elements of basketball and polo. The aim is for the teams of 4 players each, to score a goal by throwing the ball into the opponent's basket, a net suspended three yards above the ground, at the end of the pitch. This is a team sport which requires perfect rapport between mount and rider and necessitates good, well trained horses who must be forward going and with similar qualities to polo ponies. They may be larger than polo ponies (size may be an advantage when it comes to catching the ball in flight) and all horse ball horses must be courageous enough to ride into a melée. This tiring game takes place on an easy-to-manage pitch (it only needs to be 60 yards long and 30 yards wide and in fact a dressage arena will suffice) and combines the fun of a ball game with the magic of working with the horse. The most sceptical spectators fall under its spell and it shows every sign of becoming more and more popular.

10

5

11

14

6  7

12

15

8

13 A fairly new sport, horse ball is a favourite with the public and riders alike. It is particularly exciting when the player reaches down to the ground (1. 7. 14) to pick up the ball with its special handles (13). Passing (2), throw ins (15) and of course scoring (16) are the highlights of the game, which may be played on ponies, too (8).

9

# FUN SPORTS

Imagination is the keynote of the horse world: since riding became a leisure activity new games and sports, each more amazing than the last, are being continually invented.

One of the most spectacular is certainly ski-joring, which combines the pleasures of skiing and equitation: skiers pulled along by horses race on snow. An explosive mixture it is only suitable for those rare adepts capable of driving a horse while also managing skis. Such winter races frequently take place in the alps, along with exciting showjumping competitions and polo matches on snow.

Ride and tie competitions started in the United States, where they were based on the famous Pony Express mail races of the last century. Ride and tie is a relay race over 16 or 32 miles, with two men to each horse. One man rides and the other runs; the mounted competitor outdistances the runner but at a certain point he has to get down, tie up the horse, which his team mate subsequently mounts, and run in his turn. Not for those who dislike too much effort!

American equitation, with its Wild West shows, happily combines dressage and showmanship. The competitors dress in clothes from the pioneer era and one immediately feels back in the Wild West. These shows are rich in events as well as in American folklore, from working the trail (getting through obstacles in front of the judges, such as opening barriers, backing over poles etc.) to "cutting out" (working cattle cowboy style) and "reining", (American style dressage). The quarter horse with its powerful hindquarters reigns supreme in these competitions: no other horse can turn on the spot as he can or so calmly stop dead and then gallop off again like lightning.

It is only recently that harness horses, too, have had their own sports. In the attempt to save threatened breeds, admirers of the heavy horse have adopted tractor racing (invented in Japan in the 1950s). Audiences at agricultural shows love to watch these massive horses pulling incredibly heavy loads

8

15

11

12 Ski-joring (2, 4, 5, 6) is the most intrepid of new equestrian sports. Western riding, using the famous Quarter Horse (2, 11) practices the equestrian skills of the cowboy (7, 9, 10, 12, 13). Tractor racing, (14) where heavy horses pull incredible loads has to be seen. Ride and run (or ride and tie as it is also called) is as exhausting for the man as for the horse (8).

9

10

13

14

# PERFORMING
# HORSES

# CIRCUS HORSES

Horses are one of the great attractions which ensure the continuing fascination of the circus, despite current trends and the lure of television, together with jugglers, bareback riders and animal tamers. Acrobatic or knowledgable, amusing or wonderful, lovable or thrilling, the horse gallops round the ring and into the imagination of the audience as does no other animal. The horse gave birth to the circus in fact. In England in 1780, Philip Astley's shows, which combined equestrian spectacles, shadow shows and acrobats, were a resounding success and were to be imitated throughout Europe. Antonio Franconi was to put the seal on the art of the circus at the Paris school of equitation in 1802, and a century later Barnum in the United States was to create the travelling circus under the big top, in the form we know it today.

In contrast to exponents of haute école, who attempt to attain perfection of movement in the horse by using the horse's own natural movements, circus trainers aimed at the spectacular. All that mattered was that a trick should evoke amazement, wonder and astonishment on the part of the audience. At a stroke the whole process of classical dressage was overturned. Whether the horse was being prepared to carry acrobats who could have absolute confidence in it, or to learn amusing or purely equestrian tricks, training became a long job in which punishment and reward alternated. Memory is a primordial sense, and the circus shows that many horses have incredible memories: obliged to learn new tricks every year for a new show, horses still exactly remember tricks learned in previous years. Sometimes hearing a particular tune is enough to set them off on a routine which may have been learnt several years before!

All kinds of horses are found in the circus, all they need is that little something extra – a quality of originality, dash and piercing intelligence – that makes a star. Even heavy horses have been used in the circus and certain breeds are particularly effective because of their colour (like the Danish Knabstrup with its black patches on a roan background, or the Appaloosan), or because of their gracefulness (like the Russian Tersky).

7

11

12

15

8

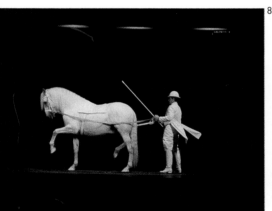

13 Horses are used in the circus in different ways: to carry jugglers (7) or other acrobats round the ring (10, 11, 13), doing tricks that imitate the actions of humans (6) and show off the horse's training. This control of the horse from the ground, at a distance (1, 6, 9) or close to (4, 8) must seem particularly amazing to an ordinary rider. Strikingly-coloured horses such as the Appaloosan (12) or the Palomino (15) are popular with circus audiences.

9

14

10

# VOLTIGE HORSES (EQUESTRIAN ACROBATICS)

S port or showmanship? Acrobatics on horseback may be both, depending whether they are being performed in a circle (legacy of the circus and military training) or in a straight line (legacy of Cossack riding).

Equestrian acrobatics performed in a circle, that is on a horse which canters continuously on the left rein around a master (who controls the horse by the aid of the voice, lunge line and schooling whip), now enjoys official competition status with a world championship for both teams and individuals. The figures in each case are quite different, teams of equestrian acrobats jump in formation, creating patterns in the air with their bodies and tumble together onto the back of a cantering horse in time to the canter. For obvious weight reasons team acrobatics are limited to young riders, and such equestrian acrobats often win world championships as young as 13 or 15 years of age. Later on, if they continue, they will go on to individual competition where, alone on the back of the horse, they perform complex routines of acrobatic movements which according to the particular test may be compulsory figures or freestyle to music. This discipline, which necessitates the qualities of a gymnast and the grace of a dancer, allied to suppleness and brilliant balance, can only be performed by someone wholly in tune with the horse. Only recently accepted as a sport, world equestrian vaulting, as it is also known, is dominated by the Germans, occasionally beaten in team events by the Swiss. The horses are chosen on the one hand for their physique – a wide, well-muscled back and even paces – and on the other for their temperament, which must be proof enough to protect the vaulter from any sudden or unexpected movement. It goes without saying that the work involved in training for voltige is enormous, requiring absolute confidence between the person on the end of the lunge, the rider and the horse. Understanding and confidence are even more important between rider and horse when practicing straight line voltige (known also as Cossack

riding) which is pure showmanship. There are many equestrian acrobats who perform straight-line voltige, often showing off their skill on a free horse, performing complex figures at the gallop!

Voltige, or acrobatics on horseback, take place as the horse moves round in a circle. The rider (5, 6, 8, 9, 11), using a strap attached to the saddle, runs along beside the horse, timing his tricks to the horse's rhythm. Teams of acrobats (12, 15) choreograph figures which are reminiscent of the circus. Straight-line voltige (1, 2, 3, 4, 7, 20, 13, 14, 16), performed on a free horse, galloping flat out, comes from Cossack riding displays.

# EQUESTRIAN STARS

The cinema could not exist without the horse, quite simply because horses are a part of life. A film about the crusades, the three musketeers, or cowboys and Indians would be impossible without putting the horse on the screen. Occasionally they succeed in making fools of the actors – when some scene turns involuntarily comic as the hero flops about in the saddle like the proverbial sack of flour. But there are many legendary scenes of horses in the cinema, from the thousands of Westerns to such films as Hitchcock's *Marnie*, in which some thoroughbred, on the racecourse of suspense, decides the course of history. The symbolism of the horse is knowledgeably used by film makers, particularly in publicity shots, where it stands for freedom, speed, integrity, country living and nobility.

As a general rule, it is professional stunt men or specialist trainers who provide directors with their four legged actors, some trained to particular tricks (many horses for example are trained to fall over, victim of a gun shot or arrow, at the squeeze of a leg). The same stunt men give incredible demonstrations of their riding prowess.

The breed of horses used will vary according to the subject of the film. In Westerns directors are particularly fond of using Indian horses in line with the characters in their pictures – which is why so many Pinto horses are seen in cowboy films. Pinto or Paint horses (depending on whether they are dark with white patches or the opposite) get their name from the Spanish word *pinto,* meaning painted.

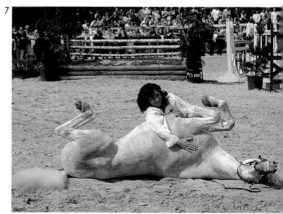

9

14

10

15

8

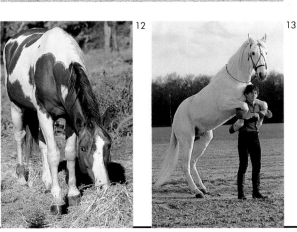

11 The film industry always needs horses, as here, filming the battle of Waterloo (14). It takes long training and understanding (3, 4, 7, 13) for a stunt rider like Marion Lurashi to carry out the stunts directors ask for (1, 2, 5), even going through fire (10). Jousting displays (6, 11) are always a great success, as is driving heavy horses (8). In an attempt to beat the record this man is driving 18 Shetland ponies (15). The Zingaro equestrian theatre, whose star is a Friesian, brings back the old style equestrian show (9). Pintos are the stars of the Western (12).

12

13

# CORRIDAS AND RODEOS

In Portugal, as in Spain, bull fighting, considered to be elevated to an art, is very popular with the public, although the rules are quite different in each country. The horse takes part in both countries but in Portugal, superbly caparisoned, plays a more important role. For a long time in Portugal bullfighting on horseback was reserved for the nobility, while the man in the street fought on foot. Rejoneadores, who face the bull on horseback, bout after bout, do not kill the bull as in a traditional corrida. But on both sides of the Iberian peninsula it is the horse that opens the proceedings, in Spain the first part is the picadors turn. Several horsemen have the job of going up against the bull before giving way to the banderilleros.

Andalusians and their marvellous Portuguese cousins, the Lusitanians (a cross between Andalusians and Arabs) make ideal bullring horses. The corrida gives the rejoneador every opportunity to use his horse's skill, courage and intelligence.

In the Wild West too the fight against the bull has given rise to spectacular competitions, among them the rodeo. In a rodeo the rider is mounted on animals primarily selected for the wildness of their bucking. More or less maltreated – at least psychologically – before the show and unable to stand a man on their back, the bucking broncos do their very best to get rid of him. The rider, who has only a single rope attached to a halter, and a saddle with no pommel to help him, has to stay on for more than ten seconds and also receives points for style. Other rodeo tests include jumping off a horse onto a bull and wrestling it to the ground.

The famous American rodeo is divided into two sections: where the rider has a saddle (5, 9, 12, 13) and riding bareback (1) – when he has to stay on for 8 seconds – an eternity. Wild West shows also include lassooing competitions (4, 6) and wagon races (2). Andalusians (7) and Lusitanians are the stars of the bull ring (11). Picadors ride horses that are trained instantly to side step out of the way of the bull (8, 10).

# SPECTACULAR TRADITIONS

The horse, daily working companion of man, has throughout the world always been associated with fetes and demonstrations. Certain traditions still exist today, in the form of equestrian spectacles which are the pride of the great riding nations and some of them are world famous. From local shows to the famous Hungarian Drive, (which consists of driving several horses single handed while standing on the backs of two of them), these sometimes brutal shows are mostly of agricultural or military origin. Among the most celebrated are the Buzkashi and the Fantasia.

Joseph Kessel's novel, *The Horsemen*, did much to spread the fascination of the Buzkashi beyond the frontiers of Afghanistan, enriched by the prose of this adventurous reporter. Originating from the nomadic tribes who guarded their sheep in the mountains, it is a wild and savage sport, not an amusing game. The aim is to fight for and carry the carcass of a goat on your saddle to a predetermined point, despite the merciless attempts of your opponents to grab the spoils themselves. In the uproar which ensues – where just about any blow is permitted – Afghan riders prove their courage, the training of their horses, and above all an ability to stay in the saddle which is often worthy of the roughest American rodeo. The Moroccan Fantasia is quite a different matter and is often the high spot of a tourist trip. The source of this tradition is military rather than agricultural. The Fantasia started in fact as a miltary exercise which allowed the riders to display their skill in the saddle (and compete against their fellows) armed with a rifle. Galloping behind their chief in a furious headlong gallop – usually directly facing the tent containing the spectators – the horsemen fire their rifles into the air and reload, shouting war cries as they charge. It is only at the last minute that they pull up in the dust, firing a last cartridge only a few yards from the spectators. The sumptuous colours and dazzling harness and costumes make this the archetypical fete of horsemen worldwide.

The Moroccan Fantasia takes place at the gallop with bloodcurdling yells and rifle shots (1, 7, 14). Riders deck the horse out from head (5, 6), to stirrup (4) to ceremonial saddle (15) and magnificence is the order of the day.

Afghan riders taking part in the Buzkashi (11, 12) are more soberly dressed (13). Melees during the Buzkashi are merciless (8) and sometimes very trying for the horses (9).

# WORKING HORSES

# A MACHINE FOR MAN

W ithout the horse what would have become of man? It has served us for transport, in agriculture, industry and every kind of activity since the dawn of time. The conquest of the horse is not only the finest conquest of man but the most useful too. The working life of horses was no sinecure. In towns, where horses moved on slipperry cobbles amongst traffic jams of carriages and riders, and later of motors too, they were worse off than in the country, where farm workers were more likely to treat them as a valued member of the family. Until the turn of the century some horses had a very hard life working down the mines, pulling heavy loads of coal and only seeing the light of day once a year – better to be a hunter, a packhorse or one used for ceremonial.

In the West the working horse has almost disappeared: where they do still work (in fields too steep for a tractor, or some vineyards, for example) they are given every care and attention and usually much affection. But elsewhere there are millions of horses who still play a vital role in man's life, earning their corn on the roads or in the fields. With the exception of black Africa, where they have virtually never been used, the Third World still turns by horsepower. Moving eastward and starting at the Middle East, donkeys and then horses gradually replace the motor car and the tractor. In Eastern Turkey there are more horse-drawn carriages than cars; in Indonesia, on the island of Java the two wheeled taxis known as *Sados* are pulled by local ponies. Tireless and willing, the indefatigable Java pony still pulls its load as it has always done.

Usually it is small horses (often of Arab or Barbary blood) or even ponies which work in these countries. Less trouble to look after, a small horse may be used in all kinds of conditions, unlike the European heavy horses. Size, too, has nothing to do with strength; look at the Icelandic ponies which have always pulled every heavy load man has required of them. In the West in the past and elsewhere still today, the horse might be called the motor of civilisation.

Horses are still around on farms (5). Working in the fields, they take part in the harvest (1, 2, 6, 8, 10) even, like these Ardennais, harvesting beetroot (3). In the developing countries as here in Turkey the horse is still the motive power of rural life (13).

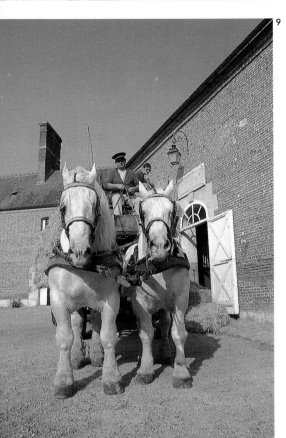

# HEAVY HORSES

The mechanisation of farming, which took place in the 1950s throughout Europe, and the invention earlier of the motor car, were a great blow to heavy horse breeds in industrialised countries. Happily, admirers of these giant, but gentle and willing horses, which had done so much for mankind, saved them from extinction.

Amongst the heavy horse breeds are the fabulous English Shire Horse with his characteristically long feathers, the biggest pure bred heavy horse in the world (many standing over 17 hands and able to pull 5 tons) and the French Percheron, a lighter and slightly smaller breed (16 hands). These two are probably the best known heavy horses but there is also the Suffolk Punch, another descendant of the Medieaval "Great Horse" on which knights rode into battle, who is famous for his exceptional pulling abilities. In Switzerland we have the lighter Franche-Montagne (sometimes also ridden), in Russia the Vladimir and in Germany the Schleswig.

10

12

13

8

9

11 The English Shire (3,6) is the largest of the heavy horses. In Belgium the Brabant still helps gather in the prawn catch (10, 13) and the Ardennais helps on the land (2, 9). Horses work, too, in big cities as in this driving demonstration in New York (2) or pulling tourist carriages in Austria (4).

The Swiss Franche-Montagne is ideal for work in the mountains (5). The Boulonnais (8) and the Breton Draught (12 ) are French heavy horses.

# WORKING WITH STOCK

Immortalised by the American cinema, the cowboy, sharing solitude and heroic deeds with his faithful four-legged companion, has become a legend. But cowboys are not just history. Despite great competition from the jeep and the helicopter they still look after and move gigantic herds of cattle in the United States (particularly on the vast plains of Texas), and their counterparts do the same for cattle and sheep in Australia. The American cowboy's favourite breed of horse is of course the quarter horse, which has no equal in the precision and skill required for cattle work. But cowboys are becoming scarcer. Being a cowboy entails not just the freedom, adventure and companionship that are so attractive, but the less enchanting daily grind of a horseman who gets down from the saddle only to carry out the everyday tasks of caring for animals, pastures and fences.

It is often forgotten that looking after stock on horseback is also a European tradition, of which the life of a guardian in the French camargue is an excellent example, carrying on the traditional way of life of their ancestors. Their methods of working and even their large black hats, short leather boots and comfortable saddles (rather like Spanish saddles) go back further even than the first American cowboys. Today, just as in the past, a guardian in the Camargue spends up to 10 or 12 hours a day in the saddle, herding the famous black bulls of the Camargue and working as part of a group, or keeping solitary watch over semi-free herds of wild horses. The number of guardians is limited, it is after all a small area, and the job is often passed down through families who have held these posts for generations. It takes nerve and exceptional horsemanship to be a guardian – as is demonstrated at such annual shows as the *ferrade*, where the cowboys of the Camargue cut out bulls from the herd.

To be a cowboy is the dream of every boy, but the helicopter is beginning to replace him (12). In Portugal (11, 14) and in the Camargue (5, 9, 13) men still look after stock on horseback and a whole festive tradition has grown out of this work. The herds themselves sometimes consist of horses as here in Hungary (4, 7).

# FORESTRY WORK

Working horses are still useful today, at the dawn of the 21st century. After some five decades of neglect, one might almost say that the horse has every chance of coming back into general working use and being essential to man once again. An example of this is the way horses are once again being used to clear fallen and cut trees. Why indeed should we bring back heavy horses to do work which tractors, much stronger and faster, can do (and requiring no more care other than to be put away afterward and filled with petrol and oil)? It is because man has become aware of the fragility of our natural environment which we have been unscrupulously ill treating since the start of the industrial era. Forestry has suffered dramatically from mechanisation: fifty years ago foresters were only able to cut a few hundred yards of wood by hand in several days work, modern tools are able to destroy acres of woodland in the same time, which would take the lifetime of a man to replace. Tractors in particular do great damage to the undergrowth; gentleness is not a characteristic of motorised clearing, as the cost of mechanisation means that fast working is essential and young saplings in the tractor's path have trouble surviving. On the other hand, working with horses allows one to take great care in clearing logs and gives one time to choose the trees to be felled more carefully, preserving those which should be preserved. In a word using horses for the work is environmentally friendly. It has never died out entirely, horses always being used in the least accessible areas. Taken to extremes mechanised wiping out of woodland results in such disasters as the destruction of the Amazon rain forests, and using the horse represents victory for the ecosystem. Pressure of public opinion, increasingly aware of environmental issues, is playing an important role in this return to traditional ways, encouraging forestry commissions to use horses instead of tractors.

8

10

9

11

Using horses for forestry work is coming back into fashion in many areas difficult of access, like these paths in the southern Alps (6) where they use Comtois mares (15). Comtois are often used (5, 6) as are Ardennais (3, 4, 11, 14) and Percherons (7). Driving these horses takes long practice (10, 12).

12

15

13

14

# MILITARY AND POLICE HORSES

Although the invention of artillery signalled the end of the direct use of the horse in battle (the First World War was to be the last in which the horse played a fighting role, other than in guerilla warfare), the horse is still very much alive in the army today. Military equitation is a tradition which does not intend to die, and army horses, often horses used for sport (many world championships are limited to military horses), still form vast legions. Although many army and police horses have disappeared throughout the world, what country does not have its prestige mounted regiment?

Among the most famous mounted police forces is that of New York, whose officers can be seen ambling along in the great city, their mounts not the least bit worried by the horrendous traffic. And of course there is a great advantage in being on top of a horse: the rider can see better and further than on foot or in a car. Canada has a notable and famous mounted police force, of course, and they often give shows of their equestrian skill. In Britain, where there is also a magnificent mounted police force, the Household Cavalry are the daily delight of excited spectators and give the greatest display of fine horses, horsemanship and tradition, wherein the horse itself is the main attraction.

Police horses need to come up to a number of standards: bought as young as possible, they are selected for size and conformation as well as colour so that they will give a uniform appearance on parade. To get them used to danger and to overcome the horse's natural tendency to fear (faced, for example, with a menacing crowd or gun shots), they are gradually trained to completely trust their rider to the extent of forgetting their instinct to run away or jib at a situation.

In parts of Europe, park and forest keepers on horseback are becoming more common. There is good reason for this professional return to using the horse in such areas, since they keep the paths clear, can be on the spot very quickly if needed, are more in keeping with the countryside and seem friendlier to walkers than police in vehicles or on foot would be.

Nearly every country in the world has its mounted regiments and police forces: Belgian mounted police (1), Italian Carabinieri (6), the Morroccan guard (4, 7). England has its famous Horse Guards (5) and mounted police, who give annual shows for the public (8), and France has its Guarde Républicaine (9, 12, 13). In North America mounted police and cavalry are very popular (2, 3), sometimes mainly for nostalgic reasons (10).

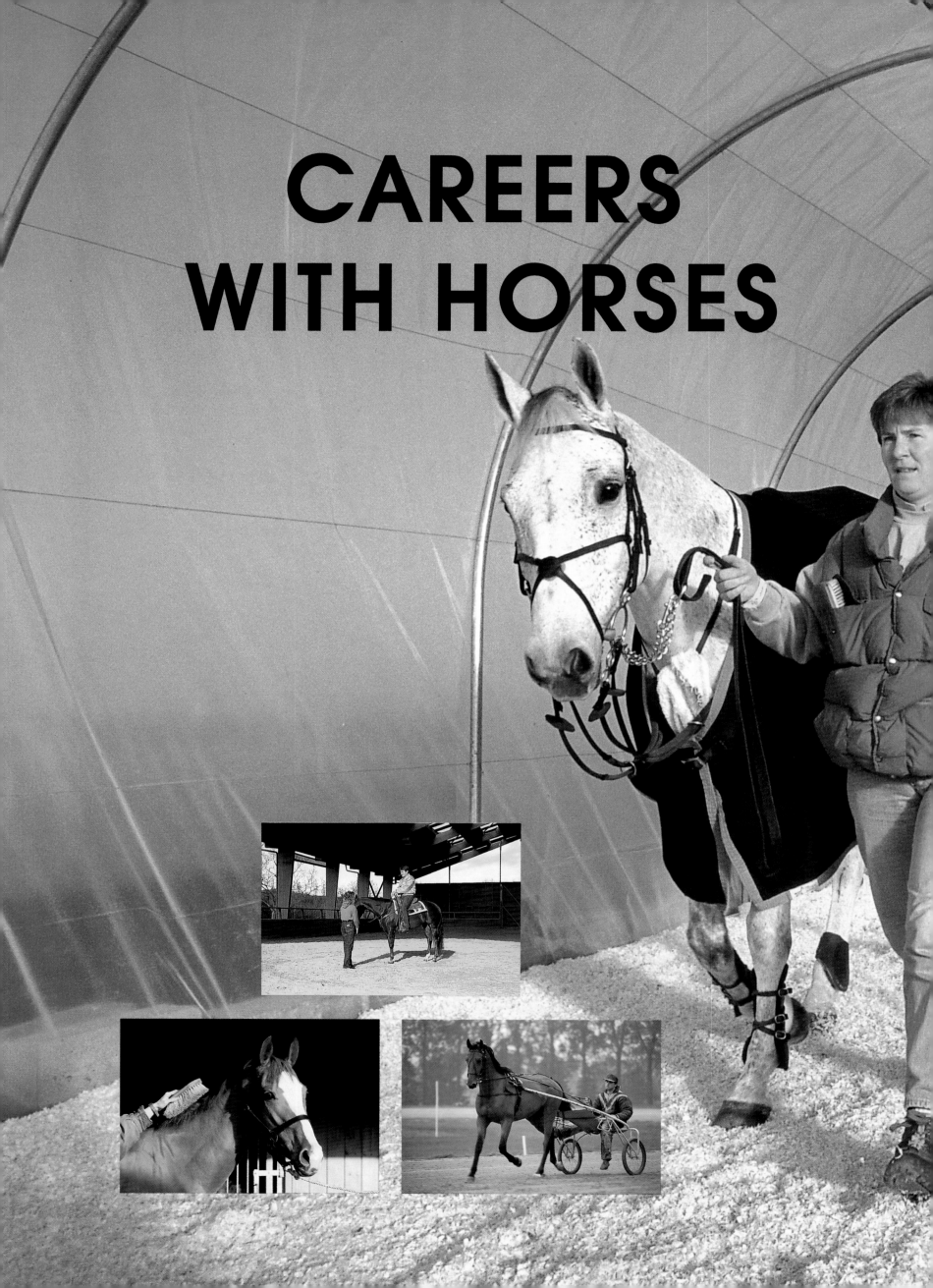

# CAREERS WITH HORSES

# BREEDERS, DEALERS AND RIDERS

**H**aving discovered and fallen in love with the horse, many young people decide to make it their career. But which direction to choose? For those who love the animal for itself the choice may be breeding; for those of a competitive spirit it may be trying to become a great rider, but it is not easy to get into the top levels of the horse world and the word "professional" is difficult to define. Is the farmer who keeps four or five brood mares a professional breeder? He certainly could not make a living from them, at any rate not in the short term. Breeding is a long-term job; most riding horses are not sold before they are 4 years old, which means five years from the mare being covered by a stallion. A great deal of patience is needed. In the world of thoroughbreds things move faster, but the sums of money involved are so great that only the rich can afford to breed bloodstock. There remains the possibility of getting a job on a stud farm; there is no predetermined training that leads to this, except that studying agronomy is advisable, since breeding relies more and more on modern techniques of selection, artificial insemination and diet, which it is essential to understand.

Professional riders stand or fall by their ability to win, which in turn depends on the quality of their horses. Since good horses are only put in the hands of successful riders this is a vicious circle which it is difficult to break (unless finance is available to buy good horses, of course). Most young people turn instead to teaching or to dealing in horses. Here, too, there is no magic path to success. You sell a horse, you negotiate for another, and bit by bit you build up a clientèle. You need an initial investment, good business sense, real horsemanship (you are going to have to tell the good ones from the bad and ride both) and a lot of integrity, to keep your clients. The profession of dealer,

with today's new leisure rider clientèle, is changing radically: shady dealers are a thing of the past. Today guarantees have to be given that you will exchange the horse if there is a problem, after sales service is essential and so is communication – full time work to be added to that of schooling and caring for the horses.

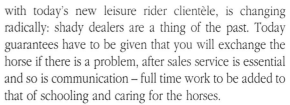

# RIDING TEACHERS AND TREKKING GUIDES

W hat greater pleasure could there be than that of passing on to children your own knowledge and passion for horses and giving your pupils a good grounding in the art of riding and respecting the horse? Teaching is said to be the best job in the world, and this is certainly true in the equestrian world. With the development of competitive riding and the increase in the number of riding centres and pony clubs, teaching has greatly evolved. For a long time it was the prerogative of the military, and methods were very strict, not to say daunting. Learning to ride and teaching methods are now open to a much more relaxed approach. Today nobody makes beginners sweat to "toughen them up"! Suddenly, as well as the equestrian skills needed to teach riding (at least to local competition standard), a basic knowledge of psychology is also required. The job of trekking guide evolved with the fashion for riding holidays. It necessitates being able to plan and carry out long trail rides, sometimes in exotic places, which have to be organised in advance in great detail. A wonderful job for those who love the fresh air and which requires as many equestrian and veterinary skills as it does qualities of tact and man management: looking after a group of people who are all strangers to each other, living in close proximity and taking part in a very testing sporting activity, can be as difficult as it is rewarding.

Finally the riding teacher, like the guide, often also runs a riding centre, perhaps as an employee of a large establishment. As manager they need to direct other employees (grooms etc.), keep the accounts, generally see that the business runs smoothly and that the clients are kept happy. Horse mad young people who go in for teaching in the hopes that it will lead to competition riding are deceiving themselves: this job is as much about looking after people as horses . But then that is part of its attraction.

# GROOMS

The people who are closest to horses are those who look after them and share their daily lives, feed them and give them affection all the time. This special relationship is evident when they are grooming a horse, carefully and vigorously brushing it over, taking a long time to pull the mane, hair by hair, or giving it that extra care which is sometimes necessary: treating a wound until it is healed, walking a sick horse, dosing it with medicine prescribed by the vet etc. And of course the stables, too, have to be looked after, boxes mucked out every day (wet and dirty bedding cleaned and changed so the horse will be comfortable), and these tasks the groom performs for only one reason: the wellbeing of the horse – who is well aware of who feeds and looks after him. Good grooms get as much back from the horse as they give to it. And so a groom who works in a competition stable and maybe looks after two or three horses has an amazing relationship with his champions, to the extent that the groom is indispensable to the stables – one has seen great horses go downhill in the absence of a beloved groom – which they never do merely on changing riders! The good groom is a very competent horsemaster in whom the competition rider may place complete confidence. Amongst his other jobs the groom has to ride the horses out at exercise or warm them up for an event as well as drive the horsebox

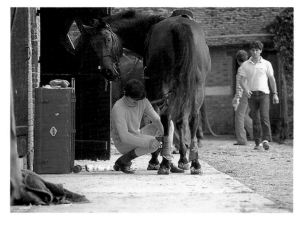

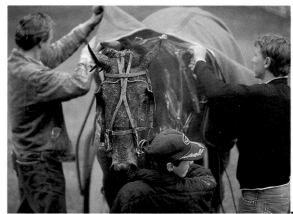

from competition to competition. Almost living the life of travelling people, grooms (often young women who are particularly suited to the caring aspects of the job) form a huge community, who in the train of their riders regularly meet up all over the world. They have in common a passion for horses which does not prevent them from preferring and boasting about their own particular charge. After a number of years of this kind of life grooms often settle down, managing a yard perhaps or moving into some different branch of the horse world where their professional experience will be of great use.

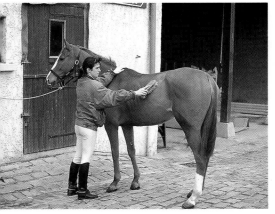

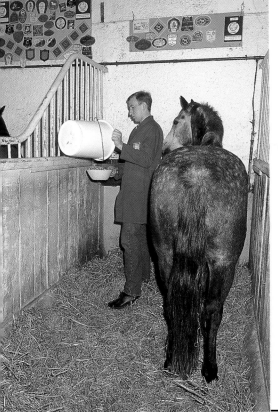

# LADS, JOCKEYS AND TRAINERS

The racecourse resounds to the noise of the crowds as the thoroughbred makes that final effort, the sleek horses thunder past ... victory! A glowing owner and trainer rush forward, the jockey gives the horse endless frenzied pats , while the cameras turn and flash ... to be that jockey is the dream of many youngsters. But too many, bitten with ambition, fight for too few places on the racecourse. Becoming a successful jockey is one of the hardest achievements in the world. But it is this dream that keeps so many apprentices in the ranks. From the age of fourteen or sixteen would-be jockeys train as apprentices; working as lads, they get up at dawn to groom their horses and muck out boxes while still going to classes. The most gifted will soon be up on a thoroughbred, riding exercise, and the best of them will perhaps one day have the opportunity to race on some provincial course. From then on it is only talent and a feeling for racing that will permit a few exceptional jockeys to attain their dream of riches and glory – provided they have not grown too tall or put on weight in the meantime  Many apprentices stay lads and some move out around the age of eighteen into new professions. But the lad, who looks after the wellbeing of the horses, is a key employee in a racing yard. A good one may go on to become head lad or travelling head lad, the trainer's right hand man at home and on the racecourse.

16

Trainers are often ex-jockeys who learn the job on the ground, although schools for trainers do exist. But no amount of learning can replace that certain natural trainer's eye, that something which makes a true wizard at training horses and jockeys; the gift which makes all the difference at the winning post.

Like racing drivers, jockeys have one of the most exciting jobs in the world.

# FARRIERS AND VETS

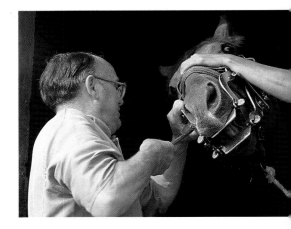

From the tips of their shoes to the tips of their teeth, horses constantly need specialist professional care. The increased interest in riding and the care with which the horse's comfort has been looked after in the last few years have revitalised the veterinary professions. They have had the same effect on the farrier's (blacksmith's) trade.

Smithing is one of the oldest equestrian professions; once king of the countryside, the farrier is no longer the pivot of village life. On the other hand farriers today do much more than merely replace the iron shoes that prevent the horse's foot from wearing out, he has also become a foot expert for the world of racing and show jumping.

Equine veterinary practitioners, too, are becoming more and more numerous. They evolved through working for studs and yards. In recent years, firstly in the exclusive world of thoroughbreds and then in the riding world in general, equine dentists have begun to appear.

Though both these professions promise rich rewards, the years of study which they undertake are daunting – becoming a vet is said to be more difficult than becoming a doctor.

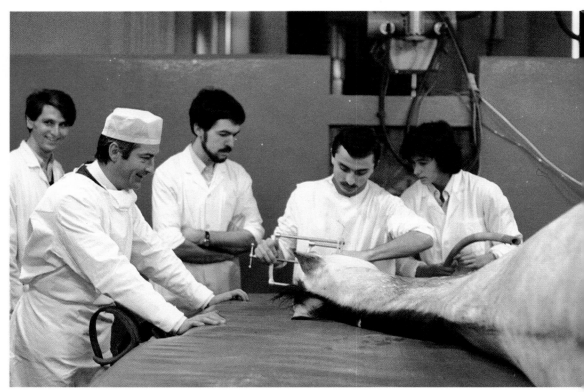

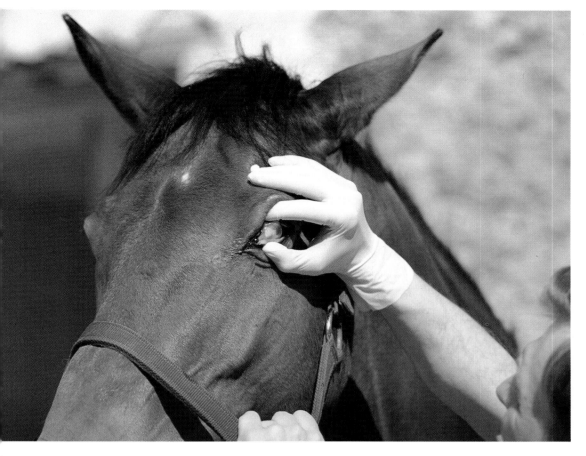

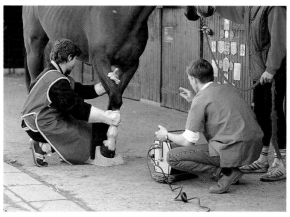

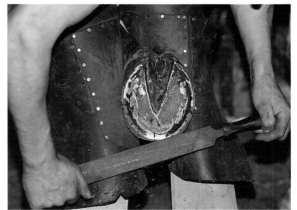

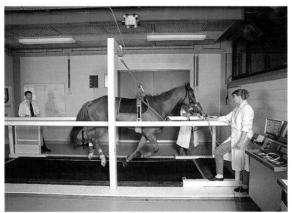

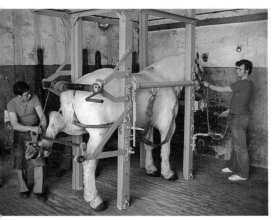

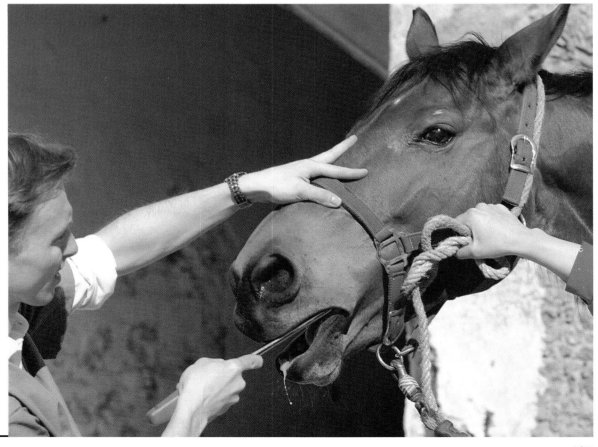

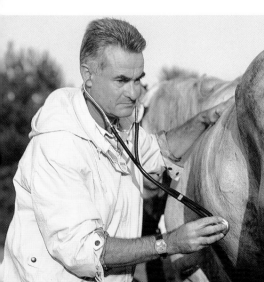

# MILITARY, SECURITY AND CAREERS ALLIED TO HORSES

In former days a young gentleman, destined for a military career, would naturally wish to become an elegant cavalry officer. Today, too, it is a desirable way of joining the army, but very few horse regiments offer the opportunity. The number of places available are far outnumbered by the prospective candidates. Only those graduating from a good military college have a hope of success.

Some specialist security firms offer jobs guarding racing yards and studs, and businesses, such as the Irish National Stud, offer a range of employment from guards (doubling as grooms and stallion handlers) to stud directors for those who have the necessary qualifications. The latter are in charge of the breeding programme, a varied and interesting job from both the scientific and management points of view.

Finally, an overview of equine careers would be incomplete without mentioning a job which, without being directly concerned with horses, is essential to the horse world. The saddler is a key craftsman who, while spending most of his time in his workshop, needs to ride regularly to try out his handiwork, be able to discuss the finer points with his clients and advise them on improvements. Journalists

and photographers who specialise in writing about and photographing horses also have entry to a world often closed to outsiders; a good grounding in basic equestrian knowledge and a good education are essentials for these careers. There are many other allied professions including animal artists specialising in painting horses. Where there is a will there is a way.

# THE HORSE

# THE FOAL'S FIRST MONTHS

In springtime, around the beginning of April, foals start to appear. Mares, after 12 months of pregnancy, often try to isolate themselves to give birth and many foals are born in the middle of the night. Breeders keep a close watch so as not to miss that magical moment when the newborn foal, who comes out head first, opens his eyes. As soon as her foal is born the mare starts to clean him by licking him all over, and thereby establishes a mutual bonding. After barely an hour, the foal (as a young horse is called until it is six months old) tries to stand on its feet, instinct urging it to be able to run away from danger, frail as its legs are. A few days later the breeder will allow mare and foal to join the others in the field, encouraging the natural herd existence. Daily becoming more confident, the foal is soon playing around its mother and, while still taking her milk, following her lead in eating grass or corn etc. Becoming a yearling at six months old (which it will continue to be called until it is eighteen moths old) it will charge around the field with its friends. Physical development will not be complete until it is three years old.

# A SYMBOL OF PRIDE AND BEAUTY

No other animal has been so much used as a symbol of beauty, grace and nobility as has the horse. Writers have compared the stance of a Thoroughbred to that of a ballet dancer, and hundreds of thousands of paintings, sculptures, poems and legends bear witness to the homage done by man to this noblest of creatures. The delicate and exquisite horse is itself a work of art.

# FREEDOM

The eternal and wonderful sight of horses at liberty is magical to watch. One could spend hours looking at horses that have been turned out into a field: playing games, galloping from one end of the field to the other, occasionally squabbling or rolling luxuriously. Gregarious animals who have always lived in herds, horses have a rich social life. They have their own language: not just neighing or whinnying but communicating by expressions of anger or trust, silent complaint or grimaces. Their ear movements play an important role in this: ears pricked forward indicate confidently paying attention, pinned back against the head they mean bad temper, and drooping indicates submission or boredom. Joy and occasionally sadness they can express as graphically as can a dog, and sudden anger can flare up between two horses for no known reason – a pair of stallions are often seen on their hind legs fighting. The way strange horses nuzzle each other or the picture of closeness given by two horses as, nose to tail, they keep the flies off each other, are all proofs of their ability to communicate in a social intercourse.

# COLOURS AND MARKINGS

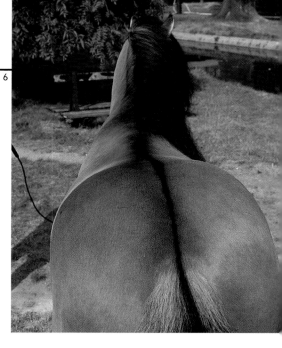

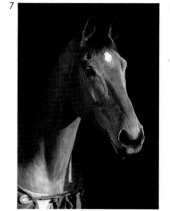

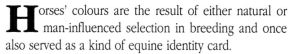

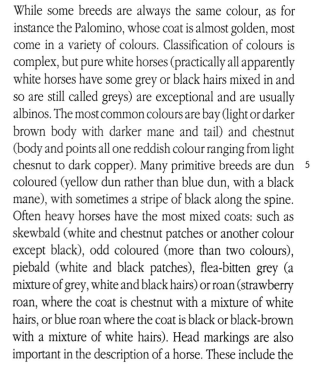

H orses' colours are the result of either natural or man-influenced selection in breeding and once also served as a kind of equine identity card.

While some breeds are always the same colour, as for instance the Palomino, whose coat is almost golden, most come in a variety of colours. Classification of colours is complex, but pure white horses (practically all apparently white horses have some grey or black hairs mixed in and so are still called greys) are exceptional and are usually albinos. The most common colours are bay (light or darker brown body with darker mane and tail) and chestnut (body and points all one reddish colour ranging from light chestnut to dark copper). Many primitive breeds are dun coloured (yellow dun rather than blue dun, with a black mane), with sometimes a stripe of black along the spine. Often heavy horses have the most mixed coats: such as skewbald (white and chestnut patches or another colour except black), odd coloured (more than two colours), piebald (white and black patches), flea-bitten grey (a mixture of grey, white and black hairs) or roan (strawberry roan, where the coat is chestnut with a mixture of white hairs, or blue roan where the coat is black or black-brown with a mixture of white hairs). Head markings are also important in the description of a horse. These include the

15

stripe, a narrow white marking down the face not wider than the flat anterior surface of the nasal bones, the blaze, a white marking covering almost the whole of the forehead between the eyes and beyond the width of the nasal bones and usually to the muzzle, and finally, the star, any white marking on the forehead. A white face means the white covers the forehead and front of the face. Tiny white markings are known as snips, and white lower leg markings are known as socks or stockings and should be accurately described for identification purposes.

12

16

17

21

22

13

18

23

19

Colours: pure white or albino horses (13) are rare. Chestnut (15) and bay (7, 8, 12) are the commonest colours. Dun (14) is a common colour among primitive breeds.

Greys (10, 23) can be any shade from very light to dark. Piebalds (black piebald: 1, or chestnut piebald: 5), and Appaloosans (9 and 11) are popular in the United States. Ardennais horses are often roan (20) and Breton draught horses sometimes yellow dun or strawberry roan (2, 18).

14

20

Markings: while the foal in photo 15 has two white stockings and two white socks, his mother only has the beginnings of white markings on her forelegs. This Arab (12) has a white stocking on his near side foreleg.

Head markings: white marking in the form of a star (7), a large star (8), star conjoined with stripe (16), and with the beginnings of a stripe (21); blaze (15, 18, 19), white muzzle (22), and white face (17).

A magnificent mule stripe (6), a marbled mouth (4) and a white patch over the croup (3).

# AMUSING HORSES

However well we think we know him, the horse is always an enigma, easily arousing our emotions and often making us laugh at the ludicrous attitudes he sometimes adopts or the strange situations we put him in; we have all seen horses playing the contortionist as they scratch their hindquarters, new born foals tangling up their unsteady legs, or stable companions gazing tenderly into each other's eyes. There is the Shetland pony who watches with glee as his rider takes a fall and the foal who

amuses himself running from one side to the other under his mother's belly.

# AMUSING HORSES

**H**orses are natural comedians and can suddenly adopt almost human expressions. Others can make us feel uneasy, like the eastern horses with lyre-shaped ears, or eyes that look as though they are made up and giving us a wink, or whose eyes have blue or light grey irises instead of the usual brown.

And they get into comic situations too, like the horse swimming across a river with only its pricked-up ears visible, the champion looking astonished as he goes up a ramp into an aircraft, or the mischievous Welsh pony gazing fearfully at the costume some pony club rider is trying to put on him. Recipient of man's generosity, too, the horse can look resplendent in the sumptuous tack in which some owner has proudly rigged him out.

# GLOSSARY

**Aids** The signals used by a rider to give instructions to his horse. The natural aids are the hands, seat, legs and voice, and the artificial aids are such items as whips, spurs, martingales etc.

**Bedding** Material spread on the floor of a stable to give the horse a dry, warm bed and non-slip floor to stand on. Traditionally straw, but wood shavings, sawdust and dried peat or bracken may also be used.

**Blood horses** General term for English Thoroughbreds

**Box** Name given to (1) an individual stable (2) vehicle used to transport horses.

**Breaking** Teaching a young horse to accept first a saddle and then a man on its back.

**Breaking out** An unnatural and unexpected sweating, even after the horse has been dried. Usually caused by over-strenuous exercise.

**Bridle** The part of saddlery that is placed over the horse's head and to which the bit and reins are attached.

**Brood mare** Mare destined to produce foals.

**Cannon bone** Leg bone of the horse that runs from knee to fetlock joint.

**Clipping out** To obviate too much sweating during exercise or work in the winter, the horse's coat is clipped to a greater or lesser degree depending on the amount of work it is expected to do.

**Collection** The horse is said to be collected when the pace is shortened by correctly raising the neck, with head position nearly vertical in conjunction with the engagement of the hind legs. The effect is to create contained power, rather like that of a coiled spring.

**Colt** An ungelded male horse under four years old.

**Conformation** The build of a horse.

**Curry comb** A metal implement with several rows of teeth (not really a comb at all) which is used to clean grooming brushes. It is never used directly on the horse.

**Dandy brush** A hard bristle grooming brush used for tough jobs, like brushing out scurf and dust from the horse's coat.

**Foal** The young horse up to the age of 12 months. Called a colt foal if it is male or a filly foal if is female

**Forehand** The part of a horse which is in front of the saddle, i.e. head, neck, shoulders, withers and forelegs.

**Forward going** A horse that steps out freely of its own accord.

**Gaits** The natural paces of the horse: walk, trot, canter and gallop.

**Gelding** A castrated male horse.

**Hand** The unit of measurement for the height of a horse, taken at the wither. One hand equals four inches.

**Impulsion** The impetus to move forward that is built up in a horse by correct use of the rider's seat, body, weight and legs and which is controlled through the reins and bit.

**Quarters** The area of the horse's body from the rear of the flank to the root of the tail and downwards on either side to the top of the leg.

**Seat** Rider's position and balance in the saddle. The action of the seat is used to give instructions to the horse.

**Sock** Lower leg marking.

**Stallion** Uncastrated male horse. Also called an entire.

**Standards** Breed characteristics.

**Stud** The establishment where horses are bred.

**Tack** Saddlery.

**Turned out** An expression meaning the horse is put into a field as against being kept in a stable.

**Vices** Faults which must be declared when selling a horse. These may be behavioural or of a medical origin and include weaving (constantly moving the head from side to side when standing in the box), windsucking (continuously and noisily pulling air down into the windpipe) and crib biting (habitually chewing mangers or doors).

**Yearling** A horse between one and two years old.

# INDEX OF BREEDS

# PICTURE CREDITS

The majority of the illustrations in this book have been drawn from the files of the Cogis picture agency, and were taken by the following photographers: Anne Amblin, Bernard Bernie, Frédéric Chéhu, Gilles Delaborde, Virginie Froidevaux, Jean-Claude Gissey, Jean-Michel Labat, Yves Lanceau, Bertrand Leclair, François Nicaise, Gérald Pottier, Charles-Pierre Rémy.
All other illustrations as follows: N. Rakhmanov/ANA 4-5; A. Storkh/ANA 82-83; Bertrand Press Agency 23; De Lis/Liaison 16-17 (16); Brissaud/Gellie/Fig Mag 34-35 (5); Haughton/Spooner 60-61 (1, 2, 9, 13); C. Vioujard 60-61 (7); E. Bouvet 62-63, 64-65 (7); C. Poulet/Gamma 64-65 (9), 90-91 (1, 6, 8, 12); Bob Thomas 64-65 (3, 5, 8, 10); Deville 72-73; Voulgaropoulos 74-75 (2); Darmigny 76-77 (3); B. De Hogues 78-79 (6, 11); PhotoNews 78-79 (14); Sallaz/Liaison 80-81 (9); M. Deville 82-83 (14); L. Dieter 82-83 (9, 11, 12, 13).

Produced by Copyright Studio, Paris
Design: Nicole Leymarie
Layout: Nathalie Boibessot
Picture Research: Veronique Cardineau
with the kind assistance of the COGIS Agency
Translated from the French by Carole Fahy
for Bookdeals Translations, PO Box 263, Taunton, Somerset